C000049610

~~BEST!~~

"SCARIEST!"

"MOST ORIGINAL!"

Whichever prize you decide to shoot for, you'll find the help you need in *The Halloween Costume Book*. Learn how easy and inexpensive it can be to make your own costume—with instructions for . . .

- ALIEN
- ASTRONAUT
- BALLERINA
- BAT
- COMPUTER
- LION

- MAD HATTER
- MAD SCIENTIST
- PRINCESS
- ROBOT
- SUPERHERO
- ZEBRA

and many more!

The Halloween Costume Book

THE HALLOWEEN COSTUME BOOK

KATHARINE THORNTON
with Illustrations by Sarah Thornton

Produced by The Philip Lief Group, Inc.

B
BERKLEY BOOKS, NEW YORK

THE HALLOWEEN COSTUME BOOK

A Berkley Book / published by arrangement with
The Philip Lief Group, Inc.

PRINTING HISTORY
Berkley edition / September 1994

All rights reserved.
Copyright © 1994 by The Philip Lief Group, Inc.
Produced by The Philip Lief Group, Inc.
This book may not be reproduced in whole
or in part, by mimeograph or any other means,
without permission. For information address:
The Berkley Publishing Group, 200 Madison Avenue,
New York, New York 10016.

ISBN: 0-425-15831-4

BERKLEY®
Berkley Books are published by The Berkley Publishing Group,
200 Madison Avenue, New York, New York 10016.
BERKLEY and the "B" design
are trademarks belonging to Berkley Publishing Corporation.

PRINTED IN THE UNITED STATES OF AMERICA

10 9 8 7 6 5 4

Love and thanks to Alice and Jim,
who introduced me first to the world
and subsequently to Halloween.

Thanks also to John, Mary Lou, Nancy, Jim, Meg,
Ned, Abby, Phil, Forrest, Irena, Margaret, Kathy, R.C.,
Eddie, Knute, Mary, Karen, Kate, David,
John, Danny, Ann, Kristin,
Linda, Frans, and Simone for their ideas and support.

And thanks to Kelli and The Philip Lief Group
and all the people at Berkley Books
for their efforts in making this book possible.

Contents

How to Use This Book 1
Chapter 1   To Sew or Not to Sew 5
Chapter 2   Foundations for Fun:
Basic Patterns 9

Basic Pattern List:
  BP #1 Skirt 10
  BP #2 Cape 11
  BP #2A Cape with Collar 12
  BP #3 Ruffle 15
  BP #4 Hood 17
  BP #5 Sleeveless Tunic 19
  BP #6 Tunic with Sleeves 20
  BP #7 Sleeveless Bodysuit 23
  BP #8 Bodysuit with Sleeves 25
  BP #9 Pom-pom 28
  BP #10 Tails 28
  BP #11 Suit of Armor 33
  BP #12 Wings 36
  BP #13 Ears 38
    • Lion and Bear 38
    • Elephant 39
    • Lamb and Monkey 39
    • Cat and Bat 40
    • Rabbit 40

CONTENTS

- Cocker Spaniel 40
- Alien and Elf 40

BP #14 Hats 41
- Witch's 41
- Clown's 43
- Crown and Tiara 45
- Chef's 47
- Robin Hood 48
- Elf's 50
- Top Hat 50
- Pillbox 53
- Turban 55

BP #15 Jacket 57
BP #16 Puffed Sleeves 58
BP #17 Petals and Leaves 59

Chapter 3   Putting It All Together 61
List of Costumes:
Alien 61
Ancient Greek Boy 62
Ancient Greek Girl 64
Angel 64
Astronaut 66
Ballerina 67
Bat 69
Bear 71
Bird 72
Boy from the Far East 73
Butterfly 75
Candlestick 75
Cat 77
Chef 78
Clown 80
Cocker Spaniel 82

CONTENTS

Computer 82
Cowboy 84
Devil 85
Die 87
Dinosaur 87
Dracula 88
Duck 90
Elephant 91
Elephant King 93
Elf 95
Fairy 96
Fairy Godmother 96
Flapper 98
Flower 99
Frankenstein's Monster 100
Ghost 101
Good Witch 103
Gypsy 104
Harem Girl 105
Henry VIII 107
Hippie Boy 108
Hippie Girl 109
King 110
Knight 112
Lamb 114
Lion 115
Mad Hatter 116
Mad Scientist 117
Magic Carpet 119
Magician 120
Mummy 122
Musician 123
Organ Grinder's Monkey 124
Pirate 125

CONTENTS

Princess 126
Queen 111
Red Riding Hood 127
Robin Hood 128
Robot 129
Rocket Ship 131
Scarecrow 133
Skeleton 134
Superhero 135
Tiger 136
Ventriloquist's Dummy 137
White Rabbit 138
Wicked Witch 140
Zebra 141

Measuring 143

THE HALLOWEEN COSTUME BOOK

How to Use This Book

Halloween has always been one of my favorite holidays because it is a time for fun, frolic, and creativity. A large part of my fondness for Halloween lies in the fact that you can create a character and wear a costume, but you don't have to learn any lines, as you would if you were in a play. There are no responsibilities or duties involved except to do no harm to yourself or others—and, of course, to have fun. This book is written to add to the fun by helping you choose and make a costume either by yourself or with your young trick-or-treater.

I have tried to write this book so that even those who have never made a costume before can produce more than sixty costumes, which are suitable for anyone from toddlers to adults. By filling in and referring to the measurement checklist in the back of the book, you can make any costume in the book in the size you require.

Each of the costumes can be made with little or no sewing. And if a little sewing is required, Chapter 1 will tell you everything you will need to know.

The Halloween Costume Book includes basic patterns in Chapter 2, which give step-by-step instructions and illustrations for making the essential elements of your costume.

You can make these basic patterns in Chapter 2 and combine them with the mask or makeup and accessories described in Chapter 3 in less than two hours.

The instructions for making each costume provide a complete list of the materials you will need and they tell you how to combine the basic patterns from Chapter 2 with a mask or makeup and accessories to create your costume. Chapter 3 will also show you your finished costume in complete detail, including mask or makeup, so you will see what you are aiming for.

How to Use This Book to Your Best Advantage:

1. The costume maker and the costume wearer should look over the alphabetically listed costumes at the beginning of the book. *Parent Alert!* Never make a costume without consulting the child. Children have strong opinions about what or who they want to be on Halloween. The costume should be a treat and part of the fun of the holiday. No one wants to see disappointment on a child's face, so select a costume with the child, keeping in mind that an early decision can save you from a frantic Halloween. October 31st is supposed to be a little scary, but not because you have nothing to wear but the same old sheet you wore last year.

I suggest you use this timetable to help you have a relaxed, happy Halloween costume making experience:

Oct. 7–11   Select the costume of your choice
Oct. 12–17   Make list and shop for materials
Oct. 18–25   Make the costume (it will take 2 hours or less)

If you are making two or more costumes, you may want to start earlier.

2. Look at the illustration of your costume in Chapter

3 so that you have an idea of what the finished disguise will look like.

3. Read the instructions on how to create your costume a couple of times. Turn to the basic patterns in Chapter 2, which are necessary to complete your costume, and read each of them carefully. If there is something you do not understand, turn to Chapter 1 and read about sewing and terms used in this book.

4. Use the measurement checklists in the back of the book to write down the measurement of the costume wearer or wearers. Measuring the Robin Hood– or princess-to-be can be educational and fun. You can have the children guess how long their arms are or how big their heads are. You can name a measurement and ask them which part of their body it describes. They can measure themselves, you, and other members of the family or friends. You can teach them about inches and feet and the fact that their feet are not two feet long.

5. Determine the amount of fabric you will need to make each of the basic patterns in Chapter 2 to make your selected costume from Chapter 3.

6. Check the list of materials you will need for your costume, including basic patterns, mask or makeup, and accessories.

7. Make a shopping list of everything you will need to complete your Halloween attire. Making your own list will insure you against time-consuming and irritating extra shopping trips.

8. Buy everything you will need to make your costume. Don't forget makeup or masks. Shopping for fabrics and other materials for your costume can be fun for your youngster, if the shopping trip is limited to the Halloween costume needs and both of you are calm and happy. No last-minute flights to the mall, please.

9. Set up all your materials and follow the easy directions in Chapter 3, referring to Chapter 2 for basic patterns when instructed to do so.

10. Consider the safety factors. Children should be able to move freely, see clearly, and manage their costumes without tripping over them. The costumes in this book should be safe for your child. Use common sense and shorten a costume if it is too long, make sure the child can see where he or she is going, and warn the child about having a safe Halloween.

If the child is trick-or-treating outdoors, warm clothing should be worn underneath the costume and strips of reflector tape should be added to the costume so that he or she can easily be seen by motorists. Have fun and enjoy the experience of costume making, which will, I hope, add to the enjoyment of you and yours this Halloween and for many Halloweens to follow.

1

To Sew or Not to Sew

If you have always been afraid of sewing and thought it was a talent only designers and some grandmothers possessed, you are in safe hands with this book. There is very little sewing involved in any of the costumes.

You can make some of the costumes in the book without sewing a stitch. You can make any costume in this book if you only know the very basics of sewing. Even if you have never considered sewing, the things you must know are explained in easy-to-follow terms.

Sewing Terms Used in This Book:

- **"Right" side** of the fabric. This is the side you want to show when the costume is finished. If you are using a printed fabric, it will be the side with the print on it.
- **"Wrong" side** of the fabric means the side that will be on the inside of your costume when it is finished.
- **Inseam** is the area of the costume that will fall against the inside leg of the costume wearer. There are two inseams in any costume that will have two legs, one on the right leg and one on the left leg.
- **Fold the fabric in half lengthwise** means that once you

5

have spread your fabric out on a flat surface with the length running vertically and the width running horizontally, you fold the fabric so that the top edge of the fabric meets the bottom edge of the fabric.

- **To fold fabric widthwise** means that once you have spread your fabric out on a flat surface so that the length runs vertically and the width runs horizontally, you fold the fabric so that the left edge of the fabric meets the right edge of the fabric.

How to Sew a Seam:

Make sure the two pieces of fabric you are joining together will stay together as you stitch. You may pin the edges together about 1½" from the edge of the fabric.

- Thread a needle with a piece of thread. Knot the ends of the thread together so the thread doesn't pull all the way through your fabric when you are sewing.
- Hold the fabric in one hand, the needle in the other and weave the needle back and forth through one side of the fabric and then through the other. Make small stitches about ½" from the outer edge of the fabric. Look, you're sewing!
- Stitch along the straight or curved line you have drawn until the seam is completed. (The basic pattern directions will explain how long the seam should be.)
- When you come to the end of the seam, turn the fabric over and sew a few stitches back over the seam you just made. Cut the thread.

That is all you will need to know about sewing to make any costume in this book.

Because children like to dress up and pretend on occasions other than Halloween, it would be nice if they had permanent collections of costumes. Sewing helps make the costumes more permanent. Therefore, if sewing a seam doesn't frighten you too much, you may want to hem all the sides of the fabric before making the costume. This means that you would add 1" to the width measurement of the fabric and 2½" to the length of the fabric. Then you would fold and pin ½" of the top and two sides of the fabric toward the wrong side and sew a seam along the edges. At the bottom of the fabric, you would fold and pin up 2" of fabric and sew a seam along the fabric where the two pieces meet. After cutting a neck hole about 1" smaller than you will need for the neck, you can make 1" slits all around it, fold in toward the wrong side of the fabric, and sew a seam around the neck of the costume. You will then have a more finished look and a more permanent costume.

2

Foundations for Fun: Basic Patterns

These basic patterns are referred to in Chapter 3 as BPs, and are numbered for your convenience. They will help you create the costume of your choice. Each basic pattern can be made in less than half an hour and requires very little sewing. All the necessary sewing instructions can be found in Chapter 1.

You will save time by filling in one of the measurement charts in the back of the book before you begin to make the basic pattern (BP) you will need for your chosen costume. You will need the measurements to determine the amount of fabric necessary for the BP. If you are making more than one, be sure to buy enough fabric for each of the patterns.

Remember that these patterns are indeed basic. Feel free to add any special touches that you think would enhance your costume. Be creative and have a fun-filled costume-making adventure.

Basic Pattern #1: Skirt

You will need:

Waist measurement
Measurement from waist to length of skirt desired
Fabric
Yarn (twice the waist measurement)
Scissors

BP #1: Skirt

To make the skirt:

1. Double the waist measurement. This will be the width of your fabric.

2. Measure the distance from the waist to the length of the skirt desired. This will be the length of your fabric.

3. Spread the fabric out on a flat surface. Draw a line with white chalk 2" from the top of the fabric along the width of the fabric.

4. Fold the fabric over along the line you have just drawn and cut ½" slits at 1" intervals along the fold. Unfold the fabric.

5. Bring the two lengths of the piece of fabric together so that the last five slits you made overlap the first five.

6. Starting with the first overlapping slit, weave yarn in and out of all the slits you have made. Push the fabric into even gathers along the yarn. Your skirt is ready to wear. Just step into it and tie it in the back of the wearer's waist.

Basic Pattern #2: Cape

You will need:

Shoulder measurement
Measurement of distance from nape of neck to the length
    of cape desired
Fabric
Heavy yarn (twice the neck measurement)
Scissors

To make the cape:

1. Double the shoulder measurement. This will be the width of your fabric.

2. Measure the distance from the base of the neck to the

length of the cape desired. This will be the length of your fabric.

3. Spread the fabric out on a flat surface and draw a chalk line about 2" from the top of the fabric along the width of the fabric. Fold the fabric on that line and cut ½" slits along the fold at ½" intervals. Unfold the fabric.

4. Take the piece of heavy yarn and weave it in and out of the slits you have made. Push the fabric into even gathers along the yarn.

5. Tie the cape loosely around the neck.

You are on your way to Halloween fun as a caped crusader or a witch.

Basic Pattern #2A: Cape with Collar

You will need:

Shoulder measurement
Measurement of distance between nape of neck and either back of knees or heels
Fabric
Piece of felt (12" × 12")
Sewing needle and thread
Heavy yarn (twice the neck measurement)
Scissors

To make the cape with collar:

1. Double the shoulder measurement. This will be the width of your fabric.

2. Measure the distance from the nape of the neck to the length of the cape desired. This will be the length of your fabric.

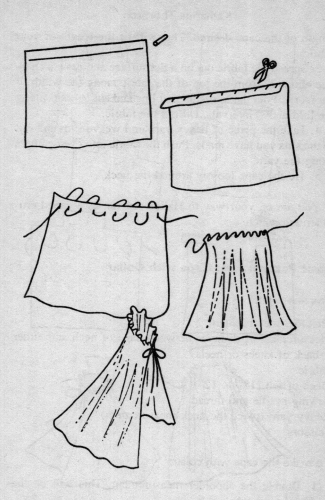

BP #2: Cape

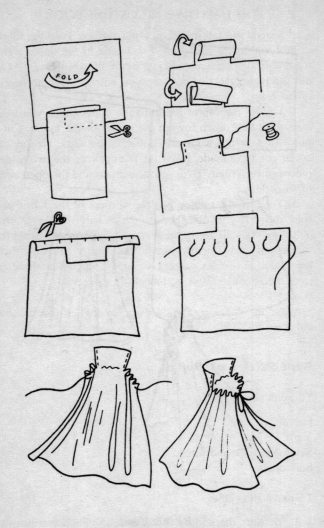

BP #2A: Cape with Collar

3. Spread the fabric out on a flat surface. Fold the fabric in half widthwise and draw a rectangle in the upper right-hand unfolded corner as shown in the illustration (2A). Cut out the rectangle, making sure you are *cutting* both *pieces of the fabric*.

4. Unfold the fabric and fold the collar piece you have created in half down toward the center of the fabric. Cut a piece of felt into a rectangle that is the same size as the collar you have made. Insert the felt between the two folded pieces of the collar. Then sew a seam around the open sides of the collar.

5. Take the two outermost top corners of the fabric and fold about 1½" of the fabric over on itself. Make 1" slits at 1" intervals all along the width of the fabric. Unfold the fabric and weave heavy yarn in and out of the slits. Push the fabric into even gathers along the yarn. Put the cape over the shoulders and tie loosely at the neck.

Wear the collar up. And adventure awaits you as Dracula!

Basic Pattern #3: Ruffle

You will need:

Fabric
Yarn
Sewing needle and thread
Scissors

To make the ruffle:

1. Measure the width of the fabric to which you want to attach a ruffle. Double that measurement. This will be the length of your ruffle fabric.

A

B

C

BP #3: Ruffle

2. The width of the fabric for a neck ruffle should be about 8". The width of the fabric for a skirt ruffle may be about 10". The width of the fabric for a wrist ruffle should be about 6". The width of the fabric for a shirtfront ruffle should be 6".

3. Draw a chalk line across the length of the ruffle approximately 1" from the top edge of the fabric. With a piece of thread the same length as the fabric on which you are

going to attach the ruffle (for a ballerina costume, use a piece of thread as long as the waist measurement plus 1"), stitch along the line you have drawn until all of the fabric is on the thread. Knot the thread and push the fabric along the thread until your ruffle is evenly gathered.

4. Attach a piece of stick-on Velcro to each end of the ruffle and fasten it around the neck or wrists. To attach to a shirtfront, stick Velcro onto the ruffle (about six small pieces spaced evenly along the length) and onto the shirtfront and fasten.

Basic Pattern #4: Rounded or Pointed Hood

You will need:

Fabric (10" × 20")
Sewing needle and thread
Yarn (14" long)
Scissors

To make the hood:

1. On a flat surface, fold the fabric in half lengthwise, making sure the right side of the fabric is inside the fold.

2. For a **pointed hood,** draw a chalk line from the fold along the length of the left side of the fabric. Sew a seam along that line and turn the hood inside out. *Skip Step 3 and continue with Step 4.*

3. For a **rounded hood,** follow Step 2 and then cut off the top left corner of your fabric as shown in Illustration #4. Sew a seam along the curve and down the length of the edge of the fabric. Turn the hood inside out.

4. Put the hood on the costume wearer and fold any excess material around the face inside the hood. Carefully

remove the hood. Then sew a seam around the folded hood opening.

5. If the hood is too long for the wearer, cut it to the desired length, knotting the end of the thread from the seam at the new length.

6. Sew a 7" piece of yarn onto each side of the hood so that it can be tied loosely around the neck.

pointed   **round**

BP #4: Rounded and Pointed Hoods

Basic Pattern #5: Sleeveless Tunic

You will need:

Shoulder measurement
Measurement of distance between nape of neck and either
    waist, mid-thigh, or back of heels
Waist measurement
Fabric

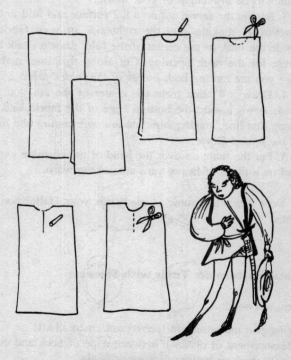

BP #5: Sleeveless Tunic

Heavy yarn (twice the waist measurement)
Scissors

To make the sleeveless tunic:

1. Add 4" to the shoulder measurement. This will be the width of your fabric.

2. Measure the distance from the base of the neck to the desired length of your tunic. For vests, measure from neck to 1" below waist. *In any case, double the measurement.* This will be the length of your fabric.

3. Spread the fabric out on a flat surface and fold in half lengthwise, making sure the right side of your fabric is inside the fold. In the center of the fold, draw a chalk half circle for the neck opening. Cut along that line, making sure you are *cutting* both *pieces of the folded fabric.*

4. Draw a 4" line from the center of the cut you just made down toward the bottom edge of the fabric, and cut along that line, making sure you are *only cutting* one piece *of the folded fabric.*

5. Put the tunic on over the head of the costume wearer and tie a piece of heavy yarn around the waist.

Your sleeveless tunic is ready for your Halloween hi-jinks.

Basic Pattern #6: Tunic with Sleeves

You will need:

Wingspan measurement (see measurement chart)
Measurement of distance between nape of neck and either mid-thigh or bottom of knee or heels

Fabric
Sewing needle and thread
Yarn
Scissors

To make the tunic with sleeves:

1. Wingspan measurement (with arms extended out to the sides, measure from fingertips to fingertips) will be the width of your fabric.

2. Measure the distance from the base of the neck to the desired length of the tunic. *Double this measurement.* This will be the length of your fabric.

3. On a flat surface, spread your fabric out and fold it in half lengthwise, making sure that the right side of the fabric is inside the fold.

4. In the center of the fold, draw a chalk half circle for the neck hole. Cut along that line.

5. From the center of the half circle, draw a 4" line down the center of the tunic. Making sure to *cut* only one *piece of the folded fabric*, cut along that line.

6. Keeping the fabric folded lengthwise, fold the fabric in half widthwise.

7. Make a chalk mark about 10" from the top of the fabric on the unfolded edge of the tunic. Measure the length of the costume wearer's arm. Draw a straight horizontal line from the mark you made toward the opposite edge of the fabric and cut along that line, making sure *to cut* all four *pieces of the folded fabric*.

8. Draw a straight line from the bottom of the tunic to the underarm of the sleeve. Cut along this line, making sure to *cut* all four *pieces of the folded fabric*.

9. Unfold the fabric widthwise (the fabric should still be folded lengthwise), and behold the shape of your tunic

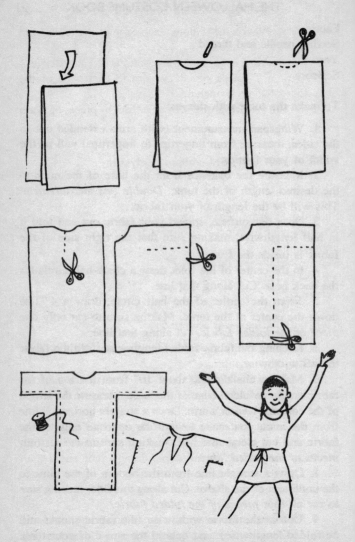

BP #6: Tunic with Sleeves

with sleeves. Sew a seam along each edge of the tunic from the bottom to the underarm.

10. Now sew a seam along the bottom of each sleeve.

11. Sew a 7" piece of heavy yarn to each side of the back slit at the neck opening.

12. When wearing the costume, tie a piece of yarn around the waist.

Basic Pattern #7: Sleeveless Bodysuit

You will need:

Shoulder measurement
Measurement from neck to heels
Fabric
Sewing needle and thread
Yarn (14" long)
Scissors

To make the sleeveless bodysuit:

1. Add 4" to the shoulder measurement. This will be the width of your fabric.

2. Measure the distance from the base of the neck to the back of the heels. *Double that measurement.* This will be the length of your fabric.

3. On a flat surface, fold the fabric in half lengthwise, making sure the right side of the fabric is inside the fold. In the middle of the folded edge, draw a half circle with chalk for the neck opening. Cut along the line you have drawn, making sure that you are *cutting* both *pieces of the folded fabric.*

4. From the center of the half circle you have just made, draw a 12" line straight down the center of the back of the fabric.

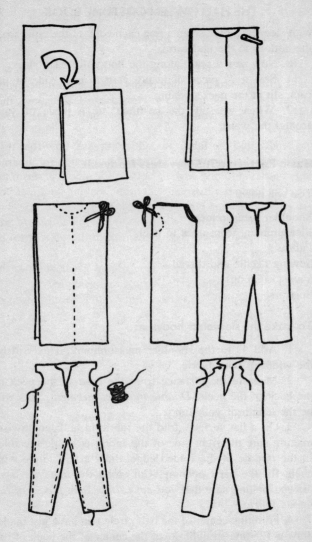

BP #7: Sleeveless Bodysuit

5. Cut along that line, making sure you are *only cutting* one piece *of the folded fabric*.

6. From the center of the bottom of the fabric, draw a chalk line upward the length of the distance from the inside of the ankle to the top of the leg (inseam). Cut along that line, making sure you are *cutting* both *pieces of the folded fabric*.

7. Keeping the fabric folded lengthwise, now fold it in half widthwise. Draw a half circle large enough for an armhole on the unfolded edge of your fabric, about 1" from the top. Cut along the line you just drew, making sure that you are *cutting* all four *pieces of the folded fabric*.

8. Unfold the fabric widthwise. *(The fabric should still be folded lengthwise.)* Sew a seam from the bottom to the top of both inseams.

9. Sew a seam up each side of the garment from the bottom of the fabric to the start of the armhole.

10. Sew a piece of yarn about 7" long to each side of the neck opening.

Turn the bodysuit right side out, and you are on your way to becoming a lion or tiger or bear. Oh, my!

Basic Pattern #8: Bodysuit with Sleeves

You will need:

Measurement from neck to heels
Measurement of wingspan
Fabric (55" width)
Yarn (14" long)
Sewing needle and thread
Scissors

To make the bodysuit with sleeves:

1. Measure from the base of the neck to the back of the heels. Add 2". *Double this measurement.* This will be the length of your fabric.

2. Measure the costume wearer's wingspan (see measurement chart). This will be the width of the fabric. (If the costume wearer's wingspan measures more than 55", you can sew another piece of fabric onto the first.)

3. On a flat surface, fold the fabric in half lengthwise so the right side of the fabric is inside the fold.

4. In the center of the fold, draw a half circle for the neck hole. Cut along the line you have drawn.

5. Draw a chalk line from the center of the half circle you just made down about 12". Making sure you are *only cutting* one *of the pieces of the folded fabric*, cut along the line.

6. Measure the distance of the costume wearer's inseam (distance from inside ankle to inside top of leg). Draw a line the length of that measurement from the center of the bottom edge of your fabric straight upward. Cut along that line.

7. Fold the fabric in half widthwise. Draw a chalk line equal to the measurement of the costume wearer's arm from fingertips to shoulder (about 10" from the top of the fabric), starting at the unfolded edge and going toward the folded edge.

8. Cut along this line, making sure you are *cutting* all four *pieces of the folded fabric*.

9. Draw a line from the underarm of the garment to the bottom edge of the fabric. Cut along this line, making sure you are *cutting* all four *pieces of the folded fabric*.

10. Unfold the fabric widthwise (it should still be folded lengthwise) and sew a seam up the length of the fabric on

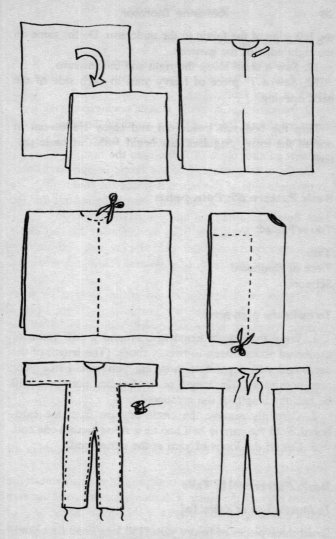

BP #8: Bodysuit with Sleeves

the left edge of the fabric to the underarm. Do the same on the right edge of the garment.

11. Sew a seam along the right and left inseams.

12. Sew a 7" piece of heavy yarn to each side of the neck opening.

Turn the bodysuit inside out and enjoy Halloween in one of the many disguises that begin with this basic pattern.

Basic Pattern #9: Pom-poms

You will need:

Yarn
Piece of cardboard
Scissors

To make the pom-pom:

1. Wrap thick yarn lengthwise around a stiff piece of cardboard about fifteen to twenty times. (The length of the cardboard will depend on how big you would like your pom-pom to be. The length of the finished pom-pom will be half the length of the cardboard.)

2. Carefully remove the circle of yarn from the cardboard. Fold the yarn in half and tie a string around one end.

3. Cut all the loops of yarn at the untied end.

Basic Pattern #10: Tails

To Make a Lion or Zebra Tail

Braid three pieces of heavy yarn (15" long) and tie a pom-pom to one end. Sew the tail onto the back of the costume.

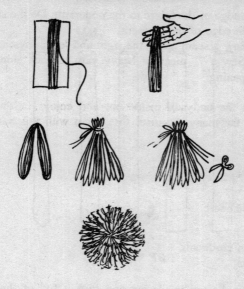

BP #9: Pom-pom

To Make a Rabbit or Bear Tail

Sew a pom-pom to the back of the costume.

To Make a Dog, Monkey, Elephant, Cat, Tiger, or Devil's Tail

1. Take a piece of fabric about 1 yard long and 3" wide. Fold the fabric widthwise so that the right side is inside the fold. Begin 1" down from the top of your fabric and sew a seam along the length of the unfolded edge. (The 1" piece of fabric you left unsewed will be the tab with which you attach the tail.)

2. For a **devil's tail,** cut one end into a double point (see illustration in Chapter 3). For all other tails, cut the end of the tail into one point. In either case, sew that end.

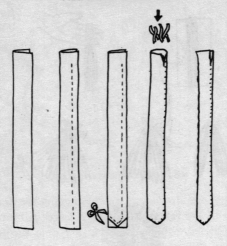

BP #10: Tail

3. Turn the tail inside out and stuff it full of shredded newspaper or cotton (see ''Attaching a Tail,'' page 32).

To Make a Dinosaur Tail

You will need:

2 pieces of green felt (18" × 24")
Poster board (18" × 24")
White chalk
Scissors
White glue
Stick-on Velcro (8")

To make the tail:

1. Glue one piece of felt onto each side of the poster board.

BP #10: Dinosaur Tail

2. Enlarge the drawing above by pinning the drawing to the center of the felt and drawing a larger tail around the outline of the drawing. Trace the tail onto the felt with white chalk. Cut along the line you have drawn.

3. Attach tab of tail onto costume with stick-on Velcro.

Cocker Spaniel's Tail

You will need:

2 pieces of brown felt or fake fur (18" × 24" each)
Poster board (18" × 24")
3" length of stick-on Velcro
White chalk
Scissors
White glue

To make the tail:

1. Glue the fake fur or felt onto each side of the poster board.

2. Enlarge the drawing and trace it onto the felt or fake fur with white chalk.

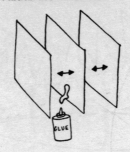

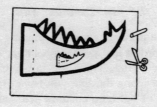

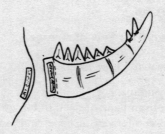

BP #10: Making a Dinosaur Tail

3. Cut out the tail and attach it to the back of the costume with stick-on Velcro.

Attaching a Tail

To attach a tail to a costume, simply stick a piece of stick-on Velcro to the tabs of the tail. Stick the receiving end of

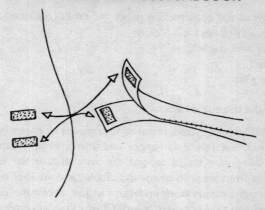

BP #10: Attaching a Tail

the Velcro onto the back of the costume. Press the two pieces of Velcro together.

Basic Pattern #11: Suit of Armor

You will need:

Shoulder measurement

Measurement from nape of neck to top of leg

Length and circumference of upper and lower arms as well as thighs and shins

Silver poster board:
    4 pieces for arm coverings
    4 pieces for leg coverings
    2 pieces for tunic

2 pieces of black netting fabric (10" × 20" each) for rounded hood (BP #4)

Sewing needle and black thread

1 piece of red construction paper for cross (optional)
24" length of stick-on Velcro
Stapler and staples
Scissors
White glue

To make the suit of armor:

1. Make four cylinders out of four pieces of poster board. One will encircle each upper and lower arm. Wrap one piece of poster board around the arm so that the length extends from wrist to below the elbow, and another so that the length extends from underarm to just above the elbow. Cut off any excess poster board. Close cylinders around the appropriate body part so that the poster board overlaps by 1" and secure it with stick-on Velcro.

2. Make two cylinders for the thighs and two cylinders for the lower legs. Thigh cylinders should encircle the area from top of leg to just above the knee; lower leg cylinders should encircle the area from the ankle to just below the knee.

3. Use two pieces of poster board to make the front piece and back piece of the suit of armor. Place one piece of poster board on top of the other piece and draw a sleeveless tunic shape (see illustration), making sure the length will cover the costume wearer from neck to upper thigh and the width is as wide as he or she is. (Remember to draw the tabs on the sides and shoulders of the tunic.) Cut out the tunic, making sure you are *cutting* both *pieces of poster board*.

4. Glue or staple the tabs on one side and one shoulder of the front piece of the armor to the tabs on one side and shoulder of the back piece. Attach stick-on Velcro to the tabs on the other side and shoulder of the front piece and the back piece so the knight can slip into his armor

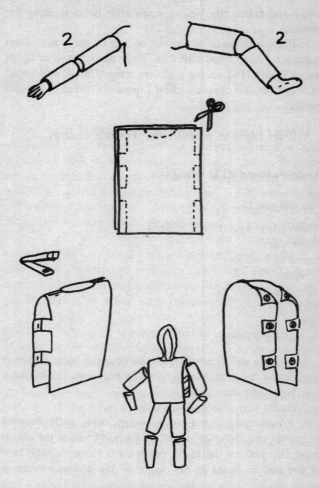

BP #11: Suit of Armor

easily and fasten the Velcro strips after he is wearing the costume.

5. Place one piece of netting on top of the other. Then make a rounded hood (BP #4). Wear black pants or tights and a T-shirt. Put on leg and arm armor, hood, and tunic. Glue cut-out red cross on chest (optional). Wear silver half mask.

You are ready to perform your knightly errands.

Basic Pattern #12: Wings

You will need:

White poster board (24" × 36")
White yarn
Pencil and eraser
Scissors
Hole puncher
White glue

To make the wings:

1. Enlarge the illustration on the opposite page. Trace it onto poster board and cut it out. Use hole puncher to make four holes in center piece.

2. Insert yarn into two top holes.

3. When ready to put on the wings, bring each piece of yarn over one shoulder, cross the yarn in front of the chest, bring the yarn to the back, insert each piece through one of the bottom holes in the center of the wings, and tie a knot.

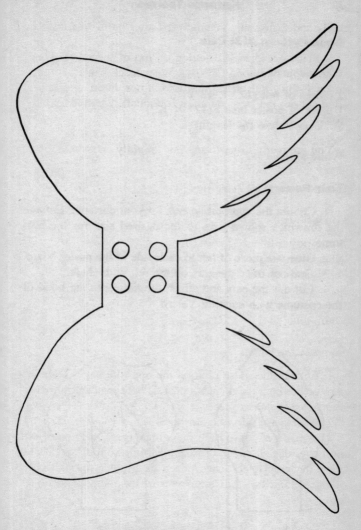

BP #12: Wings

Basic Pattern #13: Ears

You will need:

2 pieces of felt (12" × 12")
1 piece of poster board (12" × 12")
Stick-on Velcro (6" length)
Scissors
White glue

To make ears:

1. Choose the appropriate ears for your costume. Enlarge the drawings shown here to the desired size for the costume.

2. Glue one piece of felt to each side of the poster board.

3. Draw or trace the ears on the felt with chalk.

4. Cut out the ears and attach the tabs onto the hood of the costume with stick-on Velcro.

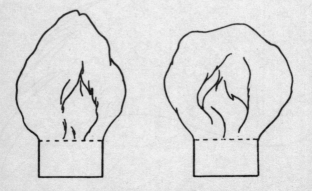

BP #13: Lion and Bear Ears

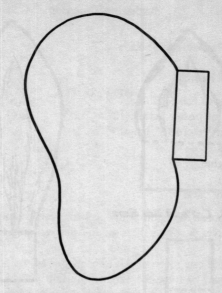

BP #13: Elephant Ears

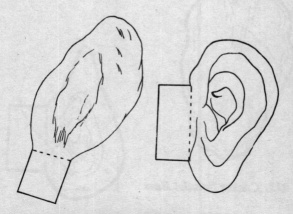

BP #13: Lamb and Monkey Ears

BP #13: Cat and Bat Ears

BP #13: Rabbit Ears

BP #13: Cocker Spaniel Ears

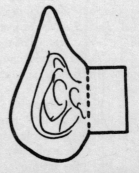

BP #13: Alien and Elf Ears

Basic Pattern #14: Hats and Other Headwear

Witch's Hat

You will need:

2 pieces of black poster board (18" × 24")
White glue
Pencil and eraser
Masking tape
Scissors

To make the hat:

1. Place one piece of poster board on a flat surface so that the 24" edges are at the top and bottom. Draw the largest half circle you can fit onto the poster board and cut it out.

2. Make this half circle into a cone shape with the point of the cone being the center point of the straight line.

3. Fit the cone to the costume wearer's head, and glue the cone together. Use masking tape to hold the glued edges together until the glue dries.

4. Take the second piece of poster board and trace the outline of the bottom of the cone onto it.

5. Draw a second circle inside the one you have just drawn, which is 1" smaller than the first. Erase the larger circle.

6. Draw another circle around the outside of the one remaining, which is 3" larger.

7. Cut out the larger circle. Then cut out the middle of the smaller circle, making a brim for the hat.

8. Place the brim over the point of the cone and let it slide down as far as it will go.

BP #14: Witch's Hat

9. Cut 1" slits along the bottom edge of the cone at 1" intervals and fold them up toward the outside of the cone.

10. Glue the strips to the underside of the brim.

Don the hat. You look bewitching!

Clown's Hat

You will need:

1 piece of bright, solid-colored poster board (18" × 24")
Pencil
Fabric for ruffle (BP #3)
Yarn for pom-poms (BP #9)
Stapler and staples
Scissors
White glue

To make the clown's hat:

1. Make a cone. (Follow Steps 1, 2, and 3 of the witch's hat instructions.)

2. Make a ruffle (BP #3) large enough to fit around the cone about 2" from the base. Glue the ruffle onto the bottom of the cone.

3. Make three 3" pom-poms (see BP #9). Attach them to the front of the clown hat. Make three vertical slits where you want the pom-poms to be and pull the tied end of the pom-pom through the hole from front of cone to inside. Secure the pom-pom from the inside of the cone with masking tape. To avoid making slits, attach the pom-poms to the hat with stick-on Velcro.

Your clown is ready for the big top.

BP #14: Clown's Hat

Crown

You will need:

A piece of poster board (18" × 24")
Pencil and eraser
Ruler
Gold foil
Costume jewelry (optional)
Scissors
White glue

To make a crown:

1. Measure the costume wearer's head. Add 1". This will be the length of the poster board.
2. The width of the poster board should be about 7".
3. Glue a piece of gold foil the same size as the poster board to both sides of the poster board.
4. Along the length of the crown-to-be, draw evenly spaced triangles as shown. Then cut along the line you have drawn.
5. Glue the two edges of the crown together. The ends should overlap by 1".
6. You may attach some costume jewelry to add richness to the crown.

Now you have a crown worthy of any member of the royal family.

Tiara

You will need:

Tinfoil (12" × 12")
Plastic headband
Scissors

BP #14: Crown and Tiara

To make the tiara:

1. Fold a piece of tinfoil over a plastic headband so the ends of the foil meet.

2. Cut slits at ½" intervals along the edge of the foil that go up to the headband.

3. Twist the strips so that they stand up.

4. Bend each strip into the design shown in Illustration #14C

Chef's Hat

You will need:

1 piece of white crepe paper (18" × 24")
1 piece of white poster board (18" × 3")

To make the chef's hat:

1. Measure the chef-to-be's head. Add 1". This will be the length of the poster board. The width of the poster board should be 3".

2. On a flat surface, spread out a piece of crepe paper 10" wide and the same length as the poster board.

3. Glue one end of the crepe paper to the poster board along the whole length.

4. Bring both ends of the poster board strip together so that 1" overlaps and glue them together.

5. Carefully bring all of the crepe paper through the center of the hatband. Bunch the crepe paper together and put a rubber band around the end (about 1" from the end).

6. Take the end and gently push the crepe paper back up through the hatband.

Your order, please?

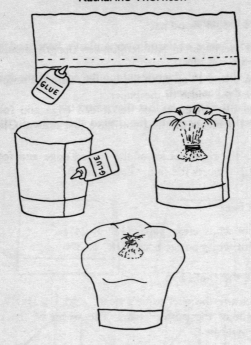

BP #14: Chef's Hat

Robin Hood Hat

You will need:

Green construction paper (16" × 14")
Pencil
A 10" piece of elastic for chin strap
Feather, either real or cut out of construction paper (12" ×
    12")
Scissors
White glue

To make a Robin Hood hat:

1. Fold the paper in half lengthwise (length should be about 14").

2. Draw a line 1" up from the bottom, with the unfolded edge across the width of the paper.

3. Take the left corner of the folded edge and fold it down until it meets the line you have just drawn. Glue it down.

4. Take the right corner of the folded edge and fold it down until it meets the line. Glue it down.

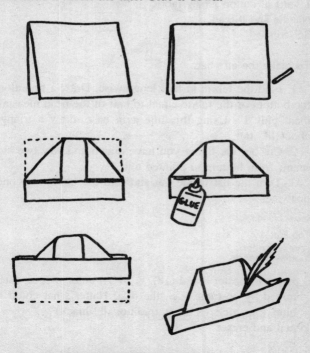

BP #14: Robin Hood's Hat

5. Fold the bottom edge of the paper up around the outside of the hat to form a brim.

6. Glue either a real feather *or* a feather made from construction paper onto the side of the hat.

Watch out for the Sheriff of Nottingham!

Elf's Hat

You will need:

1 yard of cotton jersey fabric
Needle and thread
Scissors

To make the elf's hat:

1. Fold the fabric in half lengthwise. Draw a line along the bottom of the fabric equal to half of the head measurement plus 1". Using this line as a base, draw a triangle about 14" tall.

2. Cut out the figure you have drawn and sew two side seams from bottom to pointed top.

3. Turn the hat inside out and fold the bottom up once or twice.

Top Hat

You will need:

3 pieces of poster board (18" × 24")—color will be determined by costume (i.e., the Mad Hatter's hat could be blue, a magician's hat is traditionally black)
Pencil and eraser
Scissors
White Glue

BP #14: Elf's Hat

To make the top hat:

1. Measure the costume wearer's head. Add 1". This will be the width of the poster board.

2. The length of the poster board should be 13".

BP #14: Top Hat

3. Bring the two lengths together so that they overlap by 1" and glue them together to form a cylinder.

4. Trace the end of the cylinder onto the second piece of poster board.

5. Outside the circle you have just drawn, draw a larger circle (about 3" larger).

6. Cut out the inside of the smallest circle.

7. Cut along the outside edge of the large circle. You have made the hat brim.

8. Cut 1" slits along the bottom edge of the cylinder at 1" intervals and fold the tabs up toward the outside of the hat.

9. Slide the brim over the hat to the bottom. Glue the strips to the bottom of the brim.

10. Trace the top of the hat onto the third piece of poster board. Draw a circle 1" larger than the one you just drew around the circle you have just drawn. Cut out the larger circle.

11. Cut 1" slits at 1" intervals all around the circle. Fold the tabs you have just made toward the underside of the circle. Place the circle on top of the hat and glue the tabs to the inside of the hat.

Put on your top hat and dance the night away.

Pillbox Hat

You will need:

1 piece of poster board (18" × 24")
Colorful fabric to cover one side of poster board
10" piece of elastic for chin strap
Scissors
White glue

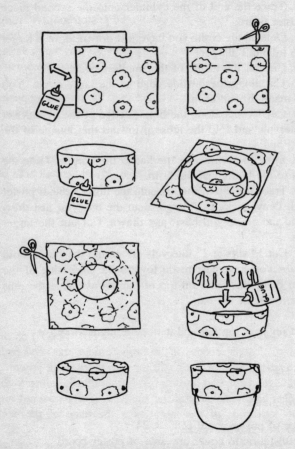

BP #14: Pillbox Hat

To make the pillbox hat:

1. Glue fabric to poster board.

2. Cut off a strip of fabric-covered poster board 4" long. The width will be equal to the measurement of the head plus 1". Bring the two lengths together so that they overlap by 1" and glue them together with the fabric on the outside of the cylinder you have formed.

3. Trace the top of the cylinder onto the remaining poster board. Draw a circle 1" large around the one just drawn. Cut out the larger circle and make 1" slits at 1" intervals all around it.

4. Fold the tabs of the circle toward the underside. Glue the tabs to the inside of the cylinder. Make a small hole on each side of the hat. Insert elastic into both holes for a chin strap.

Turban

You will need:

1 piece of lightweight fabric (10" × 60")

To make the turban:

1. Place a piece of lightweight fabric (10" × 60") on the head so that the center of the fabric covers the head from forehead to nape of neck and the two sides hang down.

2. Gather one end in each hand and pull the fabric to the back of the neck so that the head is tightly covered and twist both ends of the fabric near the nape of the neck around each other once.

3. Twist the right end until it forms a loose, ropelike strand and wrap it around the head to the left as many times as it will fit. Tuck the end securely under the last ring you have made.

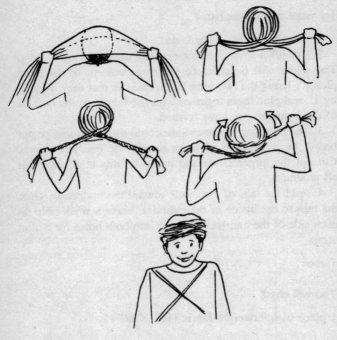

BP #14: Turban

4. Take the left end, twist it into a loose, ropelike strand and wrap it around the head toward the right side of the head until you come to the end of the fabric. Tuck the end securely under the last ring you have made.

5. Pin a brooch onto the front of the turban or glue a feather to the front of the turban (optional).

You are ready for an Arabian night of Halloween fun.

Basic Pattern #15: Jacket

You will need:

Fabric
Poster board for lapels (optional)
Fabric stiffener for lapels (optional)
Sewing needle and thread
Scissors
White glue (optional)

To make the jacket:

1. Make a tunic with sleeves (BP #6) the length of the jacket desired.
2. Turn the tunic right side out. Draw a line from bottom to top up the center of the tunic. Cut along that line, making

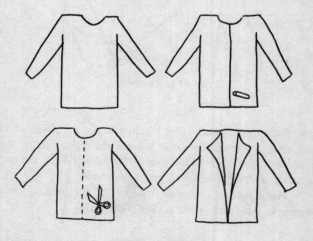

BP #15: Jacket

sure you are *cutting only* one *piece of the fabric*. Fold back the points at the top of the center cut you just made for lapels. (You may want to glue poster board or fabric stiffener to the back of the lapels.)

3. Cut the bottom to the length and shape your jacket requires. You may add buttons to the front.

Basic Pattern #16: Puffed Sleeves on Tunic or Bodysuit with Sleeves

You will need:

2 pieces of ribbon or yarn (12" × ½")

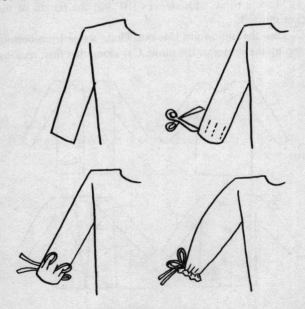

BP #16: Puffed Sleeves

To make puffed sleeves:

1. Cut sleeves of tunic or bodysuit off about 2" longer than the desired length of the finished sleeve. Make 1" holes at ½" intervals all around the sleeve, about 1" from the bottom edge of the sleeve.

2. Weave ribbon in and out of the holes. Gather the fabric into even gathers along the ribbon. Push the puffed sleeve up the arm to the desired length and tie the ribbon around the costume wearer's arm.

Basic Pattern #17: Petals and Leaves

You will need:

Poster board or crepe paper or felt (size depends on size of leaf or petal you want to make)
Pencil or white chalk
Scissors

To make petals or leaves:

1. Enlarge the illustration below and trace it onto sheets of poster board, felt, or paper.

2. Cut out the leaves or petals.

BP #17: Petal or Leaf

3

Putting It All Together

Alien

You will need:

Green fabric for tunic with sleeves (BP #6) and rounded
   hood (BP #4)
Green and black face paint
2 pieces of purple felt for ears (BP #13)
1 piece of poster board for ears
1 piece of construction paper (12" × 12") for antennae
Tinfoil for antennae
6" length of stick-on Velcro
Sewing needle and green thread
Scissors
White Glue

To make the costume:

1. Make a green tunic with sleeves (BP #6) and rounded
hood (BP #4). Place holes in hood for antennae to stick
through.

2. Make alien ears (BP #13) and attach them to sides of hood with stick-on Velcro.

3. To make antennae, roll the piece of construction paper tightly from corner to corner and form a cylinder, gluing it together. Then glue a construction-paper circle onto one end and make 1" slits in the other end to glue around a plastic headband. Repeat the process for the other antenna. Cover the antennae with tinfoil.

4. Form black circles around the eyes with black face paint.

5. Paint the rest of the face green.

Ancient Greek Boy

You will need:

White fabric for mid-thigh sleeveless tunic (BP #5)
White fabric for draped cape (20" × 40")
2 yards of gold braid or metallic tape for headband

To make the costume:

1. Make mid-thigh-length sleeveless tunic (BP #5). Use gold braid or metallic tape as a belt tied at the side.

2. Glue ends of piece of gold braid or metallic tape (head measurement plus 1") together so that they overlap by 1" and fit comfortably around the forehead.

3. Drape white fabric over one shoulder and tuck the ends into the belt at the hip on the opposite side of that shoulder. Fabric should fall loosely as in the illustration.

4. Wear sandals or ballet slippers.

You are Greek to me.

Alien and Ancient Greek Boy

Ancient Greek Girl

You will need:

White, lightweight fabric for long, sleeveless tunic (BP #5)
   and shawl (10" × 60")
2 yards gold braid
Sandals or ballet slippers
Sewing needle and white thread
Scissors

To make the costume:

1. Make sleeveless tunic (BP #5).
2. Cut off a 1½-yard strip of gold braid. Cut the strip in half. Sew one end of one half to the right shoulder of the tunic. Sew one half of the other piece of braid to the left shoulder of the tunic. Take the two pieces of braid and cross them over the chest. Then bring them to the back of the waist and cross them. Finally, bring them to the front of the waist and tie them together.
3. Attach the center of the shawl to the left shoulder of the tunic. Tuck the ends into the waistband. Put on sandals or ballet slippers. Tie ribbon or gold braid around your forehead (optional).

And you are a gracious Greek maiden.

Angel

You will need:

White fabric for tunic with sleeves (BP #6)
2 pieces of poster board (24" × 36" each) for wings (BP #12) and halo
White yarn (2 yards long)

Ancient Greek Girl and Angel

Sewing needle and white thread
Tinfoil for halo
Pencil and eraser
Hole puncher
Scissors
White glue

To make the costume:

1. Make white tunic with sleeves (BP #6).
2. Cut out wings (BP #12) from poster board and insert
yarn as described.

3. Make a halo by cutting a strip of poster board 1" wide and the length of the head measurement plus 1". Bring the ends together to form a circle and glue them so that they overlap by 1". Cut two strips 2" shorter than the first and glue one on top of the other. Glue them into a ring as you did with the first strip. Roll a piece of construction paper into a tight cylinder by starting at one corner and rolling toward the opposite corner. Glue it together.

Glue each end to the inside of one of the rings you have made. Cover the stem and the smaller ring with tinfoil. Wear the larger ring of the halo on the head, secured with hairpins.

Astronaut

You will need:

White fabric for bodysuit with sleeves (BP #8)
3 monkey tails (BP #10) made from white fabric (to be used as tubing)
Large, empty cereal box and tinfoil to cover it
2 pieces of heavy white yarn (36" long)
Shredded newspaper or cotton for stuffing tubing.
Sewing needle and white thread
Scissors
White glue

To make the costume:

1. Make white bodysuit with sleeves (BP #8) and three monkey tails (BP #10) cut into nine 12" pieces.
2. While the costume wearer is wearing the bodysuit, wrap one piece of tubing around the neck, two around each

upper arm, and two around each ankle to determine correct length needed.

3. Cut off any excess tubing. After the costume wearer removes the bodysuit, sew the tubing onto the appropriate parts of the costume.

4. Remove the top from a large, empty cereal box. Make two holes with scissors or a pencil on the back of the box about 10" from the top. Pull one end of a piece of yarn through each hole and tie the ends securely inside the box. Glue tinfoil around three sides of the box. Glue a piece of tinfoil to the front of the box. Turn the box upside down so the open end is on the bottom. When you are ready to add the backpack to the costume, cut the yarn in half so you have two "straps" coming out of the box. Bring each strap over one of the shoulders, cross them over the front of the costume, bring them to the back, and tie them.

Everything should now be A-OK for your space adventure. Happy landings!

Ballerina

You will need:

Leotard and tights
Fabric, netting, for ruffle (BP #3)
Sewing needle and thread
Stick-on Velcro
Plastic headband for tiara (BP #14)
Tinfoil for tiara
Ballet slippers (optional)
Scissors
White glue

Astronaut and Ballerina

To make the costume:

1. Make a tutu by making two ruffles. Use *only Step 3* for ruffle (BP #3). (Length of thread = waist measurement + 1", length of fabric = twice the waist measurement, width of fabric = 16".)

2. Sew two ruffles together along the gathers.

3. Attach stick-on Velcro strips to each top end of the ruffle. (One piece of Velcro will be on the right side of the fabric and one will be on the wrong side of the fabric.) Bring the ends together so that the fabric overlaps by 1" and fasten.

4. Make tiara (BP #14).

5. Wear tights, leotard, ballet shoes or flats, and the tutu. Put hair up in a bun, if possible, and don your tiara.

You are ready for your debut.

Bat

You will need:

Black long-sleeved jersey and black tights
Black fabric for cape (BP #2) and rounded hood (BP #4)
Black felt for bat ears (BP #13)
Black half mask
Scissors

To make the costume:

1. Make cape (BP #2) and scallop the bottom edge to look like bat wings by cutting half circles all along the bottom of the cape.

2. Make rounded hood (BP #4) out of black fabric.

3. Make bat ears (BP #13) and attach them to hood with stick-on Velcro.

4. Wear black tights and a black, long-sleeved jersey with hood and cape and black half mask.

Stay out of the belfry.

Bat and Bear

Bear

You will need:

Brown fabric for bodysuit with sleeves (BP #8) and rounded hood (BP #4)
Brown yarn for pom-pom tail (BP #9)
Poster board (12" × 12")
2 pieces of brown felt for ears (BP #13)
1 piece of pink felt for ears
Sewing needle and brown thread
Brown face paint
A black eyebrow pencil
Scissors
White glue

To make the costume:

1. Make bodysuit with sleeves (BP #8) and rounded hood (BP #4).

2. Make bear ears (BP #13) and attach them to hood with stick-on Velcro.

3. Make brown pom-pom (BP #9) for tail and sew it to the back of the costume.

4. Paint face with brown face paint. Paint round part of nose black. Draw a half circle with black eyebrow pencil from each side of the bottom of the nose to each side of the lips.

You are ready for a teddy bear's picnic on Halloween.

Bird

You will need:

Baseball cap
Yellow or orange kneesocks
Yellow or orange poster board (18" × 24")
Yellow bathroom tissue (1 roll)
Sweatpants and sweatshirt with hood *or* fabric for bodysuit
    with sleeves (BP #8) and rounded hood (BP #4)
Yellow gloves (optional)
White half mask
Scissors
White glue

To make the costume:

1. If you have the accessories necessary, wear sweatpants
pushed up to just below the knee and tucked into kneesocks, and a sweatshirt with hood, gloves, and a beak made
out of a baseball cap (Step 3, below). Wear hood over cap.

2. *Otherwise*, make the bodysuit with sleeves (BP #8).
Puff the legs just below knee length (BP #16), and make
rounded hood (BP #4).

3. To make a beak, cut out a poster-board triangle. The
base of the triangle should be the width of the brim of the
baseball cap. The length from base to the top of the triangle
should be about 14". Glue it onto the brim so that the base
of the triangle fits snugly against the cap where it meets
the brim.

4. To cover hood with rows of fringe, cut tissue paper
into strips about 2" long and cover the hood from one side
to the other with tissue strips. Make 1" slits at 1" intervals
along the length of the strips and glue the tissue onto the

hood. The more rows you add, the better it looks. You may also glue rows of tissue paper onto the mask.

5. Wear bodysuit with puffed legs tucked into kneesocks just below the knee, baseball cap with beak, covered by hood with ''feathers,'' half mask, and gloves.

Twick or tweet!

Boy from the Far East

You will need:

White or pale yellow fabric for the bodysuit with sleeves (BP #8)

White, lightweight fabric for turban (BP #14)

Gold fabric (8" × 1½ times the waist measurement)

Sewing needle and white thread

1 yard ribbon ½" wide

Gold braid or metallic tape (3 yards)

Costume jewelry (optional)

Stick-on Velcro (6" long)

Scissors

To make the costume:

1. Make a white or pale yellow bodysuit with sleeves (BP #8).

2. Puff the sleeves and legs (BP #16). You should not cut either the arms or the legs of the costume.

3. Make turban (BP #14).

4. Make a sash by wrapping the gold fabric (1½ times the waist measurement) around the waist and tying it in front.

Bird and Boy from the Far East

5. Cut the gold braid or metallic tape in half. Attach one end of each piece to the back of the waist of the sash with stick-on Velcro. Bring one piece over each shoulder and cross the braid or tape in front of the costume. Bring the braid or tape to the back of the waist and tie it. Tie the sash in front.

Butterfly

You will need:

Black tights
Black turtleneck jersey *or* leotard
Poster board for wings (BP #12)
Orange and black tissue paper
Black yarn
Tinfoil
Plastic headband
Black half mask (optional)
Hole puncher
Scissors
White glue

To make the costume:

1. Make wings (BP #12).
2. Cut out pieces of orange and black tissue paper and glue them onto all sides of the poster board in the design of your choice.
3. Make antennae by wrapping pieces of tinfoil around a plastic headband and molding them into antennae shapes.
4. Wear tights and leotard or turtleneck jersey. Attach wings with yarn as described in BP #12.

And flutter by as a Halloween butterfly.

Candlestick

You will need:

Black turtleneck jersey
Silver or gold fabric for sleeveless tunic (BP #5)

Butterfly and Candlestick

Yarn
1 piece of yellow poster board (18" × 24")
Blue face paint
Hole puncher
Scissors
White glue

To make the costume:

1. Make ankle-length sleeveless tunic (BP #5) out of silver or gold fabric.

2. Make flame by drawing a flame shape (see petals and leaves, BP #17) on the piece of poster board and cutting out an oval hole for the face. Punch two holes in either side of the lower part of the flame and insert yarn to be tied under chin.

3. Paint face with blue face paint. Paint area around the outside edge of the flame red.

4. Wear black turtleneck, gold or silver tunic.

With your face blue and the poster board flame yellow and red, you are a candle lighting the way to a bright Halloween.

Cat

You will need:

Black fabric for a bodysuit with sleeves (BP #8), rounded hood (BP #4), and tail (BP #10)
2 pieces of black felt for cat ears (BP #13)
1 piece of pink felt for cat ears
1 piece of poster board for cat ears
Sewing needle and black thread
18" strip of stick-on Velcro
Scissors
White glue

To make the costume:

1. Make black bodysuit with sleeves (BP #8), black rounded hood (BP #4), and black tail (BP #10).

2. Make cat ears (BP #13) and attach them to hood with stick-on Velcro strips.

3. Attach tail to back of bodysuit with Velcro strip.

Cat

4. Draw cat face, whiskers, and cat eyes with black eyebrow pencil as illustrated. Add blusher for pink cheeks.

You are now a fitting companion for any witch.

Chef

You will need:

White fabric for bodysuit with sleeves (BP #8)
White poster board and crepe paper for chef's hat (BP #14)

White face powder or cornstarch
Sewing needle and white thread
Scissors
White glue

To make the costume:

1. Make white bodysuit with sleeves (BP #8).
2. Make chef's hat (BP #14).
3. Smear white powder or cornstarch on face.

Princess and Chef

4. You may want to carry a pot with handle for your goodie bag.

Now you're cookin'!

Clown

You will need:

Brightly printed fabric for bodysuit with sleeves (BP #8) and clown hat (BP #14)
Contrasting solid color fabric for the ruffles (BP #3) on neck and hat
Yarn
Sewing needle and thread
Poster board (18" × 24")
White face paint and red face paint
Red lipstick
Black eyebrow pencil
Scissors
White glue

To make the costume:

1. Make bodysuit with sleeves (BP #8) out of brightly printed fabric.
2. Make clown's hat (BP #14) out of poster board.
3. Make two ruffles (BP #3) for the neck and hat.
4. Puff the sleeves at the wrists and the legs at the ankles (BP #16).
5. To make a clown's face, paint the face white and the round part of the nose and the cheeks red. Paint triangles over or under the eyebrows with black eyebrow pencil. Draw a big mouth from the corners of the mouth out and

Clown

down and apply red lipstick. Experiment until you have the clown face you want. You can't go wrong!

Have fun as off you go to join the circus!

Cocker Spaniel

You will need:

Brown fabric for bodysuit with sleeves (BP #8), rounded
    hood (BP #4), and tail (BP #10)
Brown fake fur or felt for the ears (½ yard)
White face paint and brown face paint
Black eyebrow pencil
Sewing needle and brown thread
Stick-on Velcro strip (12")
Scissors
White glue

To make the costume:

1. Make brown bodysuit (BP #8), rounded hood (BP #4),
and tail (BP #10.) Attach tail to back of bodysuit with stick-
on Velcro.

2. Make cocker spaniel ears (BP #13) out of brown fake
fur or felt. Attach them to hood with stick-on Velcro.

3. Make tail (BP #10) and attach it to back of costume
with stick-on Velcro.

4. Paint round part of nose black. Paint the rest of the
face brown. Draw a half circle from each side of nose to
corners of mouth with black eyebrow pencil.

Fetch yourself some delicious Halloween treats.

Computer

You will need:

2 cardboard boxes large enough to fit over the shoulders
    (one smaller than the other)

Gray or putty-colored paper to cover both boxes
Piece of black poster board (18" × 18")
Black felt tip marker
Bottle caps and small plastic whistles for knobs and
    switches
Scissors or utility knife
White glue

To make the costume:

1. Remove bottom of the smaller box. Cut hole in top of
box big enough for head to fit through.

2. Cut out a "screen" from the front of the box and glue
black poster board on the inside of the box to cover opening.

Cocker Spaniel and Computer

3. Cut out arm holes on the sides of the smaller box.

4. Place smaller box on the center of the top of the larger box and trace its outline onto the box. Then draw a 1" smaller rectangle inside the one you just drew and cut along those lines.

5. Glue the smaller box onto the top of the larger box.

6. Cover the two boxes with white paper.

7. Draw appropriate slots for disk drives on the bottom box. Glue on a "knob" next to the upper disc slot and a switch (little plastic whistles make excellent switches) next to the lower disc slot. Wear your own clothes under the costume. Eyeglasses add a nice touch.

Cowboy

You will need:

Jeans
Plaid shirt
Cowboy hat
Boots (optional)
Vest (optional)
Chaps (optional)
Black half mask (optional)
60" length of rope (optional)

To make the costume:

1. Wear jeans, plaid shirt, cowboy hat, vest, chaps, boots, and half mask. Wrap rope around belt in a coil.

2. Chaps can be made by cutting two rectangles from a bath mat or bath mat fabric that will cover the front of the legs. Then attach the tops of the rectangles to the inside of the belt with staples or stick-on Velcro.

You are ready for the Halloween rodeo.

Lion and Cowboy

Devil

You will need:

Red sweatpants and sweatshirt with hood *or* red fabric for bodysuit with sleeves (BP #8), rounded hood (BP #4), and tail (BP #10)

Black poster board for horns

Red or black half mask

Sewing needle and red thread

Scissors

White glue

Devil and Die

To make the costume:

1. Wear sweatsuit with hood. Add horns, tail, and half mask *or* make bodysuit with sleeves (BP #8) and rounded hood (BP #4).

2. Make horns by drawing two horns with tabs at bottom on poster board. Cut them out, fold the tabs toward the horn, and glue them to top of the hood on either side.

3. Make tail (BP #10) and cut the end into a double point. Attach tail with stick-on Velcro.

Have a devilishly fun Halloween.

Die

You will need:

A box that fits over the body and covers it from shoulders to mid-thigh (make sure arms can move freely)
White paper
Black construction paper
X-Acto knife
Scissors
White glue

To make the costume:

1. Use X-Acto knife to cut out a circle on the top of the box that the head will fit through. Cut out armholes on the sides of the box.
2. Cover box with white paper.
3. Cut twenty-one circles out of black paper and glue them to each side of the cube, indicating numbers one through six. Look at a die to see the pattern.
4. Put head and arms through appropriate holes.

Good luck on Halloween!

Dinosaur

You will need:

Fabric for bodysuit with sleeves (BP #8) and rounded hood (BP #4)
2 pieces green felt (18" × 24") for tail (BP #10)
1 piece of poster board (18" × 24") for tail
Green felt for ridges along back (4" wide × length from neck to tail)

Sewing needle and thread
24" stick-on Velcro
Scissors
White glue

To make the costume:

1. Make a bodysuit with sleeves (BP #8) and a rounded hood (BP #4).

2. Fold felt for ridges in half lengthwise. Cut triangular ridges along the unfolded edge.

3. Sew a seam joining the middle line down the length of the strip to the back of the costume. Then glue the two sides of the strip together.

4. Make dinosaur tail (BP #10) and attach with stick-on Velcro. Wear bodysuit with ridges, hood, and tail.

You are set for your prehistoric adventures.

Dracula

You will need:

White long-sleeved dress shirt
Black pants
Black fabric for a cape with collar (BP #2A)
Sewing needle and black thread
A piece of red, shiny fabric (6" × measurement of waist plus 1")
Hair gel
Black eyebrow pencil
Red lipstick
Cornstarch or white face powder
3" length of stick-on Velcro

Dinosaur and Dracula

Fangs purchased in a novelty shop (optional)
Scissors

To make the costume:

1. Make Dracula's cape with collar (BP #2A) out of black fabric.

2. Wear white dress shirt, black pants, and cummerbund made out of red, shiny fabric. (Fold the fabric so that the two lengths meet in the middle of the wrong side of the fabric. Stick pieces of stick-on Velcro to either end of the sash, one piece on the wrong side of the fabric and one on the right side. Wrap the sash around the waist so that it overlaps by 1".)

3. Make a large widow's peak at center of hairline at top of forehead with black eyebrow pencil.

4. Make Dracula pale with the help of white face powder or cornstarch. Gel the hair severely back away from the face.

The count is ready for his nightly adventures.

Duck

You will need:

Baseball cap
Black kneesocks
Black or white gloves (optional)
1 piece of yellow or orange poster board (18" × 24")
1 piece of white poster board for eyes
Felt tip markers to color eyes
Yellow sweatsuit with hood you may already have *or* yellow fabric for bodysuit with sleeves (BP #8) and rounded hood (BP #4)
Sewing needle and yellow thread
Scissors
White glue

To make the costume:

1. Wear yellow sweatsuit with legs pushed up to just below the knee and tucked into kneesocks *or* make yellow bodysuit with sleeves (BP #8) and cut the legs so they reach just below the knee and can be tucked into kneesocks.

2. Wear hood of sweatsuit up *or* make yellow rounded hood (BP #4).

3. Make beak for duck by cutting out a rectangle that is the same width as the brim of the baseball cap and about

Duck

14" long. Round off the two top corners so that when it's attached to the cap, it will look like a beak.

4. Glue the beak onto the brim so one end of the beak is against the cap and the other sticks out in front like a long brim.

5. Wear the hood over the cap. Make eyes out of poster board and glue them to the hood.

Elephant

You will need:

Gray fabric for bodysuit with sleeves (BP #8), rounded hood (BP #4), and tail (BP #10)

4 pieces of gray felt for elephant ears (BP #13)
2 pieces of pink felt for ears
2 pieces of poster board (12" × 12") for ears
Black or gray half mask
Gray fabric (12" × 12") for trunk
Gray face paint (optional)
Black eyebrow pencil
Sewing needle and gray thread
Karo syrup *or* spirit gum and spirit gum remover
Scissors
White glue

Elf and Elephant

To make the costume:

1. Make gray bodysuit with sleeves (BP #8), elephant ears (BP #13), rounded hood (BP #4), and elephant's tail (BP #10). Attach ears to hood and tail to back of costume with stick-on Velcro.

2. Make trunk and mask by forming a cloth cylinder shape and gluing it to the underside of a half mask. Drawing lines with black eyebrow pencil around the width of the trunk will add to the effect. Stick trunk to either side of the nose with a tiny piece of tissue paper and a dab of Karo syrup or spirit gum. (Spirit gum can be removed *only* with spirit gum remover.)

3. Paint face gray (optional).

Have tons of fun!

Elephant King

You will need:

Gray fabric for sleeveless bodysuit (BP #7), rounded hood (BP #4), and trunk (4" × 12")
Purple fabric for jacket (BP #15)
4 pieces of gray felt for elephant ears (BP #13)
2 pieces of pink felt for elephant ears
2 pieces of poster board for ears
1 piece of poster board for crown (BP #14)
1 piece of gold foil for crown
Black or gray half mask
White chalk
Sewing needle and gray and purple thread
Stick-on Velcro (12")
Gray face paint (optional)

Scissors
Karo syrup *or* spirit gum and spirit gum remover
White glue

To make the costume:

1. Make gray sleeveless bodysuit (BP #7) and rounded hood (BP #4).
2. Make elephant ears (BP #13) and attach to hood with stick-on Velcro.
3. Make purple jacket (BP #15) and sew three gold-tone buttons onto front of jacket.
4. Make crown (BP #14).

Elephant King and Fairy Godmother

5. Make elephant trunk by folding a piece of gray fabric in half lengthwise. Sew a seam along the unfolded edge. Turn it inside out and glue one end onto the inside of a gray or black half mask. Turn about 1½" of the other end inside itself and tape it with masking tape. Stick sides of trunk to sides of nose with a dab of Karo syrup or spirit gum. (Spirit gum can be removed *only* with spirit gum remover.)

Find your elephant queen and the children.

Elf

You will need:

Green fabric for tunic with sleeves (BP #6)
Purple cotton jersey fabric for elf's hat (BP #14)
Purple yarn (1½ times the waist measurement)
2 pieces tan or beige felt for elf's ears (BP #3)
Karo syrup *or* spirit gum and spirit gum remover

To make the costume:

1. Make an ankle-length green tunic with sleeves (BP #6).
2. Make a purple elf's hat (BP #14).
3. Make large elf ears (BP #13) and attach the top of each ear to the bottom of each side of the hat with Velcro. Stick the bottom of each ear onto the face with a tiny piece of tissue dipped in Karo syrup or spirit gum. (Spirit gum can be removed *only* with spirit gum remover.) Tie purple yarn around the waist.

Fairy

You will need:

Green tights
Green yarn for belt and attaching wings (BP #12)
Sewing needle and green thread
Green fabric for sleeveless tunic (BP #5)
Poster board for wings
Pencil and eraser
Scissors
White glue

To make the costume:

1. Make mid-thigh-length sleeveless tunic (BP #5).
2. Make wings (BP #12).
3. Wear tights, sleeveless tunic, wings, and ballet slippers.

Fairy Godmother

(See illustration, p. 94.)

You will need:

Fabric for cape (BP #2) and pointed hood (BP #4)
Wide ribbon (1 yard)
Sewing needle and thread (color should match cape and hood)
6" stick-on Velcro
Poster board and tinfoil for wings (BP #12)
Piece of construction paper and tinfoil (12" × 12") for wand
White face powder or cornstarch

Pink lipstick
Blusher
Stapler and staples
Scissors
White glue

To make the costume:

1. Make cape (BP #2) and pointed hood (BP #4) out of colored fabric.
2. Make wings (BP #12) and attach them to cape.
3. Make wand by rolling a piece of construction paper

Fairy

into a tight cylinder and covering it with tinfoil. Staple a
foil-covered poster-board star to one end.

4. Powder hair that will show with hood on. Wear cape
(kept closed with stick-on Velcro) and hood and tie ribbon
into a bow around the neck. Add lipstick and blusher.

Take up your magic wand and create a magical Halloween!

Flapper

You will need:

Knee-high stockings or stockings that can be rolled down
    to below the knee
Shiny fabric for sleeveless tunic (BP #5)
3 yards of fringe
Piece of fabric (2" × measurement of head plus 1") for
    headband
Brooch (optional)
Long strand of beads (optional)
Sewing needle and thread
Scissors
White glue

To make the costume:

1. Make sleeveless, mid-thigh-length tunic (BP #5) and
sew side seams from bottom to underarm.

2. Sew three rows of fringe around the bottom of the
tunic.

3. Make headband by wrapping strip of fabric around the
head so that the ends overlap by 1" and securing them with
stick-on Velcro. Attach a brooch to side of headband (optional).

4. Wear tunic, headband, and knee-high stockings or stockings that you have rolled down to just below the knee.

Charleston the night away!

Flower

You will need:

Green tights
Green fabric for tunic with sleeves (BP #6) and rounded hood (BP #4)

Flapper and Flower

½ yard yellow felt for petals (BP #17)
½ yard green felt for leaves (BP #17)
Sewing needle and green and yellow thread
White chalk
Blusher
Lipstick
Hole puncher
Scissors
White glue

To make the costume:

1. Make ankle-length tunic with sleeves (BP #6) and rounded hood (BP #4) from green fabric.

2. Cut out ten to twelve petals (BP #17) from yellow felt and glue the tabs of the petals onto the rounded hood, around the face opening.

3. Make eight to ten green felt leaves (BP #17) and glue them around the neck of the tunic.

4. Make two green felt leaves (BP #17) large enough to cover hands. Punch two holes in the center of the leaf and insert green yarn through each opening. Tie the yarn around the costume wearer's middle finger.

5. Apply blusher and lipstick.

Now you are fit for any garden.

Frankenstein's Monster

You will need:

A suit of clothes that are too small for you
Paper bag that fits over the head
Felt for alien ears (BP #13) (optional)
2 champagne corks or bottle tops

Black felt tip marker
White paint
Gray paint
Large shoes or boots
Scissors
White glue

To make the costume:

1. Make paper-bag mask by painting the bag white, drawing a crew cut hairdo around the top of the bag, and drawing eyes, eyebrows, nose, and mouth on front of bag. Cut out holes for eyes, nose, and mouth. Draw ears on both sides of the bag or glue on alien ears (BP #13). Make sure openings are large enough for costume wearer to see and breathe easily.

2. Paint champagne corks or bottle tops gray to resemble nuts and bolts. Glue them to either side of the ''neck'' of the paper bag mask.

3. Wear clothes that are too small, paper-bag mask, and heavy shoes or boots.

Go out and scare the townspeople.

Ghost

You will need:

White long-sleeved shirt
1 white twin bed sheet or white fabric
Black face paint
Black felt tip marker
White yarn (twice the waist measurement)
Scissors

Frankenstein's Monster and Ghost

To make the costume:

1. Put sheet over head and lightly mark where eye holes, nose hole, mouth hole, and arm holes should be. Remove the sheet and cut out eye holes, nose hole, mouth hole, and arm holes. Make sure openings are large enough for costume wearer to see and breathe easily.

2. Paint circles around eyes, nose, and mouth with black face paint. Color circles around the eye holes, the nose hole, and the mouth hole on the costume with black marker.

3. Wear a white long-sleeved shirt under the costume. Tie a piece of white yarn loosely around the neck to hold costume in place. Tie another piece of the white yarn around the waist.

4. Cut fabric or sheet to ankle length for safety.

Have a hauntingly good Halloween!

Good Witch

You will need:

Lightweight fabric for waist-length tunic with sleeves (BP #6) and ankle-length skirt (BP #1)

Ribbon (1 yard ½" wide and 1 yard 4" wide)

Gold foil and poster board for crown (BP #14)

Construction paper and foil for magic wand (1 piece each 12" × 12")

Sewing needle and thread

Red lipstick

Blusher

Scissors

White glue

To make the costume:

1. Make short-sleeved tunic with sleeves (BP #6) and puff the sleeves (BP #16) just above the elbow using narrow ribbon.

2. Make full, long skirt (BP #1) from same fabric.

3. Make crown (BP #14).

4. Wrap the wide ribbon around the waist and tie it in the back in a bow.

5. Carry a magic wand made from a cylinder of construction paper (12" × 12") rolled from corner to corner with a poster-board star glued or stapled to one end and the whole covered with gold foil.

6. Add lipstick and blusher.

Enjoy your powers!

Gypsy

You will need:

Colorful full skirt, vest, and white blouse *or* fabric for skirt
  (BP #1) and sleeveless tunic (BP #5), scarf *or* fabric
  for scarf, and large loop earrings
Boots (optional)
Red lipstick
Blusher
Black eyebrow pencil

Gypsy and Good Witch

Sewing needle and thread
Scissors

To make the costume:

1. Make the skirt (BP #1), and a vest from a sleeveless tunic (BP #5) with the center front cut open and neck cut into a V shape.

2. Wear skirt, blouse, vest, boots, loop earrings, sash around waist, and lots of jewelry and beads. Apply lipstick and blusher.

3. Fold large scarf into a triangle, wrap around head, and tie to one side.

Dance, gypsy, dance.

Harem Girl

You will need:

Lightweight, shiny fabric for bodysuit (BP #8) and veil (12" × 12")
Sewing needle and thread
Yarn or ribbon (1 yard)
Costume jewelry necklace and loop earrings (optional)
Ballet slippers or flats
Black eyebrow pencil
Lipstick
Blusher
6" length of stick-on Velcro
Scissors

To make the costume:

1. Make bodysuit with sleeves (BP #8) out of lightweight, shiny fabric and puff the sleeves and legs of the costume (BP #16) at the wrists and ankles.

2. Take length of ribbon (1" longer than head measurement) and attach a 1" stick-on Velcro strip to each end (one piece will be on the wrong side of the ribbon and one will be on the right side). Wrap the ribbon around the head and fasten it at the back with stick-on Velcro.

3. Mark the ribbon over each ear and remove the ribbon. Sew the right top corner of the veil fabric to the underside of the ribbon where you have made a mark. Sew the left top corner of the fabric to the underside of the ribbon where you have made the other mark.

4. Draw lines extending out from the eyes and curling as shown in the illustration. Add lipstick and blusher.

Your harem girl is ready for an Arabian Halloween night.

Henry VIII and Harem Girl

Henry VIII

You will need:

Black opaque tights
Purple fabric for jacket (BP #15)
2 yards black velvet for pants and hat
½ yard of white felt or fake fur for trim
Heavy purple yarn for belt
Gold pendant (optional)
Feather for hat (optional)
Sewing needle and black and purple thread
Scissors
White glue

To make the costume:

1. Make jacket (BP #15) 4" longer than torso measurement. Fold back the top two corners of the front opening to resemble lapels. Cut fake fur or white felt to the same shape and size as the lapels and glue the fake fur or white felt to that area.

2. Make hat out of velvet by cutting the fabric into hat size (width of the fabric = 1½ × head measurement, length = 14"). Fold the fabric lengthwise with the right side of the velvet inside the fold. Turn up 1" of the velvet around the bottom edge. Sew the top of the turned-up fabric to the fabric it is turned up against, like a hem. Insert yarn into the opening of the hem and pull it through the hem of the fabric until the two ends meet. Sew a seam along the right and left sides of the folded fabric, starting about 1" up from the bottom and ending at the fold at the top of the velvet. Turn the hat right side out and push the velvet into even gathers along the yarn. Put the hat on the costume wearer

and tie the yarn to the left side. Arrange the top of the hat so that it falls to the left side of the head.

3. Take a piece of velvet twice the waist measurement and long enough to cover the waist to mid-thigh. Follow Steps 3 and 4 from cape (BP #2) on both the top and bottom of the velvet so you have a piece of velvet gathered at the top and bottom.

4. Bring the ungathered edges together and sew a seam from bottom to top, making sure the yarn is not hindered by the seam and can still be pulled through the slits easily.

5. Take the crotch piece and sew one end to the bottom of the back of the costume and the other to the front. Turn the pants right side out. When Henry VIII is ready for court, have him step into the pants and pull the two ends of the bottom yarn together and tie them at the top of the leg. Stuff the pants with tissue or shredded newspaper so they puff out, and tie the two ends of yarn at the waist.

6. Wrap purple yarn around the waist of the jacket and tie it in the back. Arrange the bottom of the jacket to look like a ruffle or peplum.

7. Draw beard with black eyebrow pencil and darken eyebrows with eyebrow pencil. Wear tights, balloon pants, jacket, and hat. Add a pendant around the neck and a feather to the hat (optional).

Hippie Boy

You will need:

Pair of jeans or bell-bottom pants
Brightly printed shirt or tie-dyed T-shirt
String of long beads
Cloth headband
Clogs (optional)

Hippie Boy and Hippie Girl

To make the costume:

1. Wear pants, shirt, beads, headband around forehead, and clogs.

What's happenin', man?

Hippie Girl

You will need:

Long, printed dress
Strand of long beads
Flowers for hair
Clogs (optional)

To make the costume:

   1. Wear dress, beads, flowers in hair, and clogs.

   Love and peace.

King

You will need:

White opaque knee-highs
White, shiny fabric for sleeveless bodysuit (BP #7)
Navy blue shiny fabric for jacket (BP #15)
1 yard gold braid or metallic tape
4 goldtone buttons (optional)
Gold poster board or poster board and gold foil to cover
   for crown (BP #14)
Sewing needle and white and blue thread
Scissors
White glue

To make the costume:

   1. Make sleeveless bodysuit (BP #7) with legs that stop 2" below the knee out of white shiny fabric. Puff legs just below the knee (BP #16) and insert the bottom of the legs of the costume into the top of the opaque knee-highs. Tie a piece of gold braid around the top of each knee-high (optional).

   2. Make jacket (BP #15) out of shiny blue fabric (waist-length in front; knee-length in back).

   3. Make crown (BP #14) out of gold poster board or poster board covered with gold foil.

   4. Glue or sew goldtone buttons to the front of the jacket.

5. Glue gold braid or metallic tape to edge of jacket lapels.

6. Make three loops of gold braid and sew them onto each jacket shoulder (see illustration).

7. Wear sleeveless bodysuit, knee-highs, jacket, and crown. Add a pendant (optional).

Queen

You will need:

Fabric for tunic with sleeves (BP #6)
Metallic tape, ribbon, or gold braid (2½ yards)

King and Queen

Poster board and gold foil for crown (BP #14)
Costume jewelry necklace and earrings
Sewing needle and thread
Scissors
White glue

To make the costume:

1. Make tunic with sleeves (BP #6).
2. Sew one end of the metallic tape, ribbon, or gold braid to the right shoulder of the costume so that it hangs down the front of the tunic. Sew the other end to the left shoulder of the costume. Cut the tape, ribbon, or gold braid in half. Cross the two pieces in front and bring them around to the back of the waist and tie in a bow.
3. Tie a piece of ribbon, metallic tape, or gold braid around each upper arm, just above the elbow, and make a bow.
4. Make a crown (BP #14).
5. Add makeup and jewelry.

Your queen is ready for her royal duties.

Knight

You will need:

Shoulder measurement
Measurement from nape of neck to top of leg
Length and circumference of upper and lower arms as well as thighs and shins
Silver or gray poster board:
     4 pieces for arm coverings for suit of armor (BP #11)
     4 pieces for leg coverings for suit of armor
     2 pieces for tunic for suit of armor

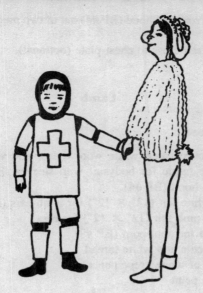

Knight and Lamb

2 pieces of black netting fabric (10" × 20" each) for
  rounded hood (BP #4)
Sewing needle and black thread
1 piece of red construction paper for cross (optional)
24" length of stick-on Velcro
Stapler and staples
Scissors
White glue

To make the costume:

1. Make suit of armor (BP #11) out of silver or gray
poster board.

2. Make rounded hood (BP #4) out of two pieces of black netting.

3. Glue red cross to chest-plate (optional).

Lamb

You will need:

White wool sweater, white wool tights, and white hood, *or* white fabric for bodysuit with sleeves (BP #8) and rounded hood (BP #4)
2 pieces white felt (12" × 12") for lamb ears (BP #13)
1 piece of pink felt (12" × 12") for ears
White yarn for pom-pom (BP #9)
Sewing needle and white thread
1 package of white crepe paper
Black face paint
Red lipstick
Black eyebrow pencil
Stick-on Velcro (6")
Scissors
White glue

To make the costume:

1. Attach lamb ears to hood and tail to white tights. Wear sweater, tights, and hood *or* make white bodysuit with sleeves (BP #8) and rounded hood (BP #4).

2. Cut crepe paper into five 3" × 20" strips. Place strips on top of one another and cut 1½" slits at 1" intervals all along one length of the strips, making sure you are cutting *all five* strips. Glue the strips onto the hood in rows starting at the hood opening and placing each strip close to the

other. Gently squeeze the tabs of each strip into curls to look like lamb's wool.

3. Cut the rest of the crepe paper into 3"-wide strips long enough to encircle the torso of the bodysuit. Cut 1½" slits at 1" intervals along one edge of the strips and glue them in rows around the torso. Gently squeeze the tabs into curls to look like lamb's wool.

4. Make pom-pom tail (BP #9) and sew it to the back of costume.

5. Make ears (BP #13) and attach them to the hood with stick-on Velcro.

6. Paint end of nose black. Draw a line from each side of nose to edge of mouth with eyebrow pencil. Apply red lipstick to mouth.

Lion

(See illustration, page 85)

You will need:

Tan or light brown fabric bodysuit with sleeves (BP #8) and rounded hood (BP #4)

Yellow yarn for pom-pom (BP #9) and tail (BP #10)

Sewing needle and tan thread

2 pieces of brown felt and 1 piece of poster board for lion ears (BP #13)

Blusher

Black eyebrow pencil

4 spools of yellow or brown gift-wrapping ribbon that can be curled

Scissors

White glue

To make the costume:

1. Make a bodysuit with sleeves (BP #8) and a rounded hood (BP #4) out of tan fabric. Add lion's mane by sticking thirty curled strands of 12"-long gift-wrapping ribbon to a piece of stick-on Velcro (about 10" long) and attaching it to the top front of the hood. Make two rows this way. Place the second row in back of the first. Add another strip around the neck of the costume (optional).

2. Braid three pieces of heavy yarn together and attach a pom-pom (BP #9) to one end for tail (BP #10). Sew the other end of the back of the costume.

3. Add blusher to cheeks, make whiskers with black eyebrow pencil, and draw a line from under the nose to the upper lip. Draw two flatted U shapes above the lips (see illustration on p. 85).

Remember, you are the king of the jungle.

Mad Hatter

You will need:

3 pieces of red or blue poster board for top hat (BP #14)
Black or blue pants
Large white shirt with collar
Blue jacket *or* fabric for jacket (BP #15)
Colorful vest *or* fabric for vest made from sleeveless tunic (BP #5) with center front cut open and V neck cut in front
A striped tie
Sewing needle and blue thread
White powder or cornstarch
Blusher

Square of poster board (2" × 4")
Black felt tip marker
White glue
Scissors
White chalk

To make the costume:

1. Make top hat (BP #14).
2. Find a jacket *or* make one (BP #15).
3. Find *or* make vest from sleeveless tunic (BP #5) cut up the center of the front and with the neckline cut into a V shape.
4. Dust hair and eyebrows with white face powder or cornstarch. Add a little blush to the cheeks.
5. Wear shirt with collar up, vest, pants, jacket, tie, and top hat.
6. Print "In this style ^{10}%" with marker on the 2" × 4" piece of poster board and glue it to the hat for an authentic Mad Hatter look.

Enjoy the tea party.

Mad Scientist

You will need:

White fabric for tunic with sleeves (BP #6)
Tinfoil (24" × 24")
Pants and shirt
Hair gel
Black ballpoint pen
Black eyebrow pencil
Blusher

Mad Hatter and Mad Scientist

To make the costume:

1. Make a white tunic with sleeves (BP #6) and slit it up the middle so it looks like a lab coat.

2. Gel or tease the hair so it looks like it never gets combed.

3. Make eyeglasses out of tinfoil by squeezing four pieces of tinfoil into four strips and bending two of them into circles and two of them into the eyeglass stems. Wear them on your head.

4. Wear pants, a shirt, the lab coat, and the glasses. Blacken and thicken the eyebrows with black eyebrow pencil.

5. Write some formulas like $E = MC^2$ on the sleeves of the lab coat with ballpoint pen. (For a crumpled look, roll the lab coat up in a ball before wearing it.)

Invent a wonderful Halloween for yourself!

Magic Carpet

You will need:

White tights
White fabric for turban (BP #14) (10" × 60")
2 paisley bath towels or paisley-printed terry cloth (26" × 46") each
2 pieces of fabric facing (26" × 46")
1 piece of poster board (12" × 12")
Stapler and staples
Masking tape
Scissors

To make the costume:

1. *Make sure towels or fabric are the right length for your costume wearer. If too long, cut to appropriate length.*
2. Press fabric facing to wrong side of each towel or piece of fabric.
3. Cut two strips of poster board each measuring 1" × 4".
4. Make shoulder straps by turning the towel or fabric to the wrong side. Staple one end of each poster-board strip to the bath towel or fabric 1" down from the top of the towel or fabric, 10" in from the outer edge.
5. Staple the other ends of the poster-board strips to the wrong side of the other towel or piece of fabric, 10" from the outer edge and 1" from the top. Cover the staples with

masking tape to prevent the magic carpet from scratching its occupant.

6. Put magic carpet over the head so the shoulder straps rest comfortably on the shoulders.

7. Make a turban (BP #14) out of white cloth. Wrap turban.

You are all set to fly to the moon and back the old-fashioned but magical way.

Note: Parents, please make sure that your child understands that he or she and the magic carpet are not capable of real flight. No flying will be allowed on Halloween or at any other time.

Magician

You will need:

Black pants
White dress shirt
Black fabric for cape with collar (BP #2A)
3 pieces black poster board for top hat (BP #14)
Needle and black thread
Black construction paper and white paint for wand
Black eyebrow pencil
Red lipstick
Blusher
Scissors
White glue

To make the costume:

1. Make long cape with collar (BP #2A).
2. Make top hat (BP #14).

Magic Carpet and Magician

3. Make wand by rolling the black construction paper into a tight cylinder. (Roll from corner to corner.) Cut off points at ends and paint tips of ends white.

4. Apply makeup.

5. Wear black pants, a white dress shirt, the cape and hat, and carry the wand.

Abracadabra! You are a magician!

Mummy

You will need:

White pants or tights
White fabric (3 or 4 yards) *or* a twin bed sheet
Black and white face paint
Masking tape
Scissors
6" stick-on Velcro

Mummy and Organ Grinder's Monkey

To make the costume:

1. Cut or tear fabric into 4"-wide strips. Use masking tape to connect one end of each strip to the next strip. Wear white pants or tights. Wrap the strips around the entire upper body, arms, and legs. Leave the waist to top of legs unwrapped, allowing the pants or tights to be pulled down low enough for access to toilet necessities. Secure last end of the strips with stick-on Velcro. Make sure strips are loose enough around the joints so that costume wearer can move freely.

2. Wrap head, leaving face exposed. With face paint, paint face white with black circles around the eyes, nose, and mouth.

3. Rub some dirt or brown chalk on the costume (optional).

Now rise to wander the Halloween night.

Musician

(See illustration, page 137)

You will need:

Black fabric for jacket (BP #15)
Sewing needle
Black thread
White felt
Black felt
Black felt tip marker
Straight-edge ruler
Glitter
Scissors
White glue

To make the costume:

1. Make black jacket (BP #15).

2. Cut white felt in the shape of two lapels and glue them to the lapels of the jacket.

3. Use a marker and a ruler to draw eight keys of a piano keyboard on each lapel. Make smaller black keys out of black felt and glue them onto the keyboard where appropriate. (One between the first two keys, one between the second and third keys, one between the fifth and sixth keys, one between the sixth and seventh keys, one between the seventh and eighth keys.)

4. Cut out white felt notes and a G clef. Cover them with glitter and glue them onto the back of the jacket.

5. Wear pants, a white dress shirt, and your musician's jacket.

Enjoy your Halloween gig!

Organ Grinder's Monkey

You will need:

Brown fabric for bodysuit with sleeves (BP #8), rounded
    hood (BP #4), and monkey tail (BP #10)
Piece of poster board for pillbox hat (BP #14)
Piece of colorful fabric for pillbox hat
2 pieces brown felt for monkey ears (BP #13)
1 piece of pink felt for monkey ears
Brown yarn
Sewing needle and brown thread
White chalk
Scissors
White glue

To make the costume:

1. Make a brown bodysuit with sleeves (BP #8), rounded hood (BP #4), and monkey tail (BP #10).

2. If you cannot find a suitable hat, make the pillbox hat (BP #14).

3. Make up face by painting it brown with face paint and adding lines from bottom, outer edge of nose to outer edge of mouth on each side of the face with black eyebrow pencil.

4. You may choose to use a vest from the accessories you have collected, or you can easily make one from the sleeveless tunic (BP #5). Cut a V neckline in the front of the tunic and cut a slit up the front center.

Pirate

(See illustration, page 135)

You will need:

Blue denim jeans
Striped long-sleeved jersey
Scarf
Sash for waist
Loop earring

To make the costume:

1. Wear jeans, shirt, scarf wrapped around head and tied on the side over the ear, and loop earring.

2. Apply blusher to cheeks and draw stubble on cheeks with eyebrow pencil.

Princess

(See illustration, page 79)

You will need:

Lightweight fabric for tunic with sleeves (BP #6)
2 yards of fabric in contrasting color for sash and skirt puffs
Sewing needle and thread
18" length of stick-on Velcro
Plastic headband and tinfoil for tiara (BP #14)
Costume jewelry necklace and earrings (optional)
Lipstick and blusher
Scissors
White glue

To make the costume:

1. Make ankle-length tunic with sleeves that end 2" above the elbow (BP #6). Puff the sleeves (BP #16). You may also change the neckline by cutting 1" slits at 1" intervals all around the neck and folding the tabs back along the wrong side of the fabric. Then sew a seam along the neckline.

2. Make a sash out of contrasting fabric (6" × 36") by folding it along the length on each side, in toward the center of the wrong side of the fabric.

3. Cut remaining piece of contrasting fabric in half lengthwise. Sew four corners of one piece together and then to the underside of the sash above the right hip. Sew the four corners of the other piece of fabric to the underside of the left side of the sash above the left hip. The two pieces of fabric will fall over the hips of the costume wearer when the sash is put around the waist and tied at the back.

4. Tie the sash around the waist and make a bow in the back.

5. Make a tiara (BP #14).

6. Put on gown, sash with puffs, and jewelry. Fix costume wearer's hair in a bun or upsweep, if possible. Put on the tiara.

7. Apply lipstick and blusher.

Red Riding Hood

You will need:

White blouse and tights
Red fabric for cape (BP #2), pointed hood (BP #4), and ankle-length skirt (BP #1)
Sewing needle and red thread
Red lipstick

Red Riding Hood and Robin Hood

Blusher
Scissors
Basket to carry goodies (optional)

To make the costume:

1. Make red, ankle-length skirt (BP #1), cape (BP #2), and pointed hood (BP #4).

2. Wear skirt, white blouse, white tights, cape, and hood and carry a trick-or-treat basket.

Watch out for wolves!

Robin Hood

You will need:

Dark green or dark brown tights
Dark brown fabric for sleeveless tunic (BP #5)
Green construction paper for Robin Hood hat (BP #14)
Piece of green or brown poster board (18" × 24") for quiver (arrow carrier)
Brown or green heavy yarn
6 pieces brown construction paper (12" × 12") for arrows
1 piece of black poster board for arrowheads (12" × 12")
Black eyebrow pencil
Blusher
Scissors
White glue

To make the costume:

1. Make brown sleeveless tunic (BP #5) and Robin Hood hat (BP #14).

2. Make quiver as follows:

   a. Bring two lengths of the poster board together so they form a cylinder and overlap by 1" and glue the edges together.

   b. Make a hole on either side of the cylinder about 2" from the top. Insert a piece of yarn (2 yards long) in one hole and knot it on the inside of the cylinder. Insert the other end of the yarn into the opposite hole and knot it inside the cylinder. Gently stretch the yarn so it is taut and cut it in half.

   c. When Robin Hood is ready for his Halloween adventures, put one piece of yarn over each shoulder like a strap. Cross the straps in front of the chest and tie the two ends behind the waist.

3. Make arrows as follows:

   a. Roll pieces of brown construction paper into narrow cylinders by taking one corner of the paper and rolling it toward the other corner. Glue the corner to the paper underneath it. Cut off the points at both ends.

   b. Cut poster board arrowheads (triangles will do) and glue them onto arrow shafts you have just made. Put the arrows (heads up) into the quiver.

4. Draw a beard with black eyebrow pencil (see illustration) and add some blusher on the cheeks for a rugged, outdoorsy look.

Robot

You will need:

Shoulder measurement

Measurement of length and circumference of arms (upper and lower) and legs (thighs and calves)

Measurement of distance from neck to top of legs
Measurement of width of upper body at the widest point
White pants and T-shirt
White poster board:
    4 pieces for arm coverings
    4 pieces for legs
    2 pieces for tunic
1 box large enough to fit head and white paper or white
    paint to cover it
1 large empty cereal box and white paper to cover it
12" square of black netting fabric
24" length of stick-on Velcro
Four bottle tops or black felt tip marker for dials
Stapler and staples
Scissors
White glue

To make the costume:

    1. Follow Steps 1 through 4 for the suit of armor (BP #11).

    2. Take a box that fits comfortably over the head of the robot-to-be. Cut a 4" strip of poster board the length of the costume wearer's head plus 1" and cut 1" slits at 1" intervals all along one edge. Bring the ends of the strip together so that the ends overlap by 1". Center the headband in the bottom of the inside of the box and glue the tabs of the headband to the box. Staple one end of a 10" piece of elastic to each side of the headband to be used as a chin strap. This will make the box more comfortable for the wearer. You may also want to fill the inside of the head-band area with a layer of cotton or felt.

    3. Cut out a square (large enough for the face to show) on the front of the box. Glue black netting over that opening on the inside of the box.

4. Cover the outside of the box with white paper or paint it white.

5. Cover the cereal box with white paper and glue it to the front of the tunic. Glue on bottle tops to simulate controls.

Wear white pants and T-shirt under costume for best effect. Put on poster-board arms, legs, and tunic. Place head box carefully on head.

Program yourself to have a happy Halloween.

Rocket Ship

You will need:

3 pieces of white poster board (24" × 36" each)
Stickers of American flag (optional)
Orange crepe paper
Masking tape
Stapler and staples
Scissors
White glue

To make the costume:

1. Draw the largest half circle you can fit onto one piece of poster board. Cut it out.

2. Make a cone out of the half circle of poster board using the center of the straight edge as the point of the cone. Glue the cone together. Use masking tape to hold the cone together until the glue sets.

3. Staple the other two pieces of poster board together to form a cylinder that will fit the costume wearer's body.

4. Place the cone on top of the cylinder and use eight pieces of masking tape to tape them together on the inside.

Reinforce the tape by stapling each end of each piece you used.

5. Place the rocket ship over the costume wearer's head and mark the place where the face hole and armholes should be. Remove the costume and cut out an oval for the face hole and cut two circles for the armholes.

6. Cut large leaves (BP #17) out of crepe paper to resemble fire from the ignition and glue them to the inside of the bottom of your spacecraft so they hang down from the rocket ship.

7. Glue stickers of a flag onto the rocket ship or paint the letters NASA on the side (optional).

8. Place rocket ship over the head of the costume wearer.

Blast off to a happy Halloween.

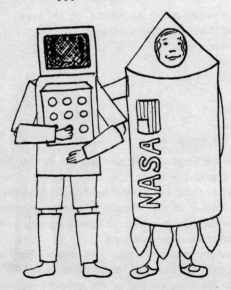

Robot and Rocket Ship

Scarecrow

You will need:

Large pair of pants
Belt or piece of rope for waist
Large shirt
Felt or straw hat *or* yellow or black felt for Robin Hood
    hat (BP #14)
Shredded newspaper or yellow crepe paper
36" length of yarn
Red face paint or blusher
Stapler and staples

Scarecrow and Skeleton

Masking tape
Scissors

To make the costume:

1. Put on large pants and shirt and stuff the arms and legs with shredded newspaper or crepe paper so that some hangs out at the wrists, ankles, and neck. Tie a piece of yarn around each wrist and ankle so the stuffing doesn't fall out. Use belt or tie a piece of rope around the waist.

2. Staple some crepe paper or shredded newspaper to the inside of the hat so that it hangs out of the hat. Cover the staples with masking tape.

3. Paint the end of the nose and cheeks red.

Keep those crows away from your candy corn.

Skeleton

You will need:

Black fabric for bodysuit with sleeves (BP #8) and rounded
   hood (BP #4)
Picture of a skeleton
White paint for cloth
White and black face paint
Paintbrush
Makeup sponge
Sewing needle and black thread
Scissors

To make the costume:

1. Make bodysuit with sleeves (BP #8) and rounded hood (BP #4) out of black fabric.

2. Paint skeleton onto front of suit with white paint. (Copy from picture of skeleton.)

3. Paint face white. Paint black circles around the eyes, nose, and mouth.

4. Wear bodysuit, hood, and face makeup.

Superhero

You will need:

Tights
Long-sleeved jersey shirt
Short shorts or bathing trunks
Fabric for cape (BP #2)

Pirate and Superhero

Heavy yarn
Half mask
Scissors

To make the costume:

1. Make cape (BP #2).
2. Wear tights, shirt, shorts, or bathing trunks and cape.

Save your metropolis from the forces of evil.

Tiger

You will need:

Tiger-striped fabric for bodysuit with sleeves (BP #8),
    rounded hood (BP #4), and tiger tail (BP #10)
Yellow felt for ears (12" × 12")
Black felt tip marker
Yellow, black, and white face paint
Needle and yellow thread
Stick-on Velcro
Scissors
White glue

To make the costume:

1. Make tiger-striped bodysuit with sleeves (BP #8),
rounded hood (BP #4), and tail (BP #10). Attach tail to
back of costume.

2. Make yellow tiger ears (BP #13). Draw black stripes
with felt tip marker and attach them to hood with stick-on
Velcro.

3. Draw a line from the center point under the nose to
the top of the lip and make two flattened U shapes at the
bottom of the line. Paint black and yellow stripes on face

Tiger and Musician

starting at the point of the chin and going toward the edges of the face in a V shape (see illustration).

Burn bright in the forest of the night on Halloween!

Ventriloquist's Dummy

You will need:

Plaid shirt
Blue jeans
Black eyebrow pencil
Blusher
Red lipstick

To make the costume:

1. Wear jeans, plaid shirt, and make up face to look like a dummy by drawing lines with eyebrow pencil from corner of mouth to underside of chin on both sides of the face. Add blusher for rosy cheeks. Put on lipstick and dot the nose and upper cheeks gently with eyebrow pencil to indicate freckles.

White Rabbit

You will need:

White fabric for sleeveless bodysuit (BP #7) and rounded hood (BP #4)

2 pieces white felt for rabbit ears (BP #13)

2 pieces white poster board (18" × 24")

1 piece of pink felt for rabbit ears

Purple fabric for jacket (BP #15)

White yarn for pom-pom (BP #9)

Large pocket watch, real *or* homemade out of poster board and gold foil

Blue poster board for top hat (BP #14)

Colorful silk or rayon scarf for bow tie

White face paint

Pink face paint

Black eyebrow pencil

Gold ribbon or yarn to hang pocket watch either around the neck or from one side of the jacket to the other

White chalk

Scissors

White glue

To make the costume:

1. Make the bodysuit with sleeves (BP #8), rounded hood (BP #4), and pom-pom for tail (BP #9). Attach tail to back of bodysuit or jacket.

2. Make rabbit ears (BP #13).

3. Make jacket (BP #15) waist-length in front and knee-length in back. Cut a 12" slit up the back and cut each half of the fabric into points to create tails.

4. Apply white face paint. Paint round part of nose pink. Draw jowls with black eyebrow pencil by making lines

Ventriloquist's Dummy and White Rabbit

from bottom of nose to upper lip on each side of face. Draw whiskers.

   5. Wear white or gray gloves (optional).

And don't be late for Halloween fun.

Wicked Witch

You will need:

Black fabric for long tunic with sleeves (BP #6) and cape (BP #2)

Wicked Witch

Three pieces black poster board for witch's hat (BP #14)
Sewing needle and black thread
Green face paint
Red fake fingernails (optional)
Black eyebrow pencil
Scissors
Stapler and staples
White glue

To make the costume:

1. Make long tunic with sleeves (BP #6) and long cape (BP #2) out of black fabric.

2. Make witch's hat (BP #14) out of black poster board.

3. Paint face green and darken eyebrows with black eyebrow pencil. Add an eyebrow-pencil mole with hair growing out of it (optional).

4. Wear red fake nails (optional).

Have a wickedly good time.

Zebra

You will need:

Black-and-white zebra-striped fabric for bodysuit with
   sleeves (BP #8) and rounded hood (BP #4)
2 pieces black felt and 1 piece of poster board (12" × 12"
   each) for zebra ears (BP #13)
Sewing needle and thread
Black eyebrow pencil
Black and white face paint
Black yarn for tail (BP #10) and pom-pom (BP #9)
Scissors
White glue

Zebra

To make the costume:

1. Make a bodysuit with sleeves (BP #8) out of striped fabric, or white or black fabric with the stripes painted onto the bodysuit.

2. Make a rounded hood (BP #4) out of same fabric.

3. Make zebra ears (BP #13) and tail (BP #10) and attach ears and tail to costume.

4. Paint black and white stripes from chin to forehead. Paint end of nose black.

Measuring

Each basic pattern in Chapter 2 requires you to measure certain parts of the costume wearer's body. If you measure all of the body parts necessary for any costume before you begin and write them in the spaces provided, you will be able to make the costume with or without the costume wearer being present.

Head measurement: _____

Neck measurement: _____

Shoulder measurement (distance from left shoulder to right shoulder): _____

Wingspan (with arms extended out to the sides, measurement from fingertips to fingertips): _____

Waist measurement: _____

Length of torso (distance from neck to waist): _____

Chest measurement (distance around chest): _____

Distance between base of the neck and mid-thigh: _____

Distance between base of neck and bottom of back of knee:

_____

Distance between base of neck and back of heels: _____

Shin length measurement (distance from bottom of knee to ankle): _____

Thigh length measurement (distance from top of leg to top of knee): _____

Width of shin (distance around shin): _____

Width of thigh (distance around thigh): _____

Upper arm (distance around upper arm): _____

Arm measurement (distance from shoulder to fingertips):

_____

Wrist measurement (distance around wrist): _____